AF606648

Mel Bochner

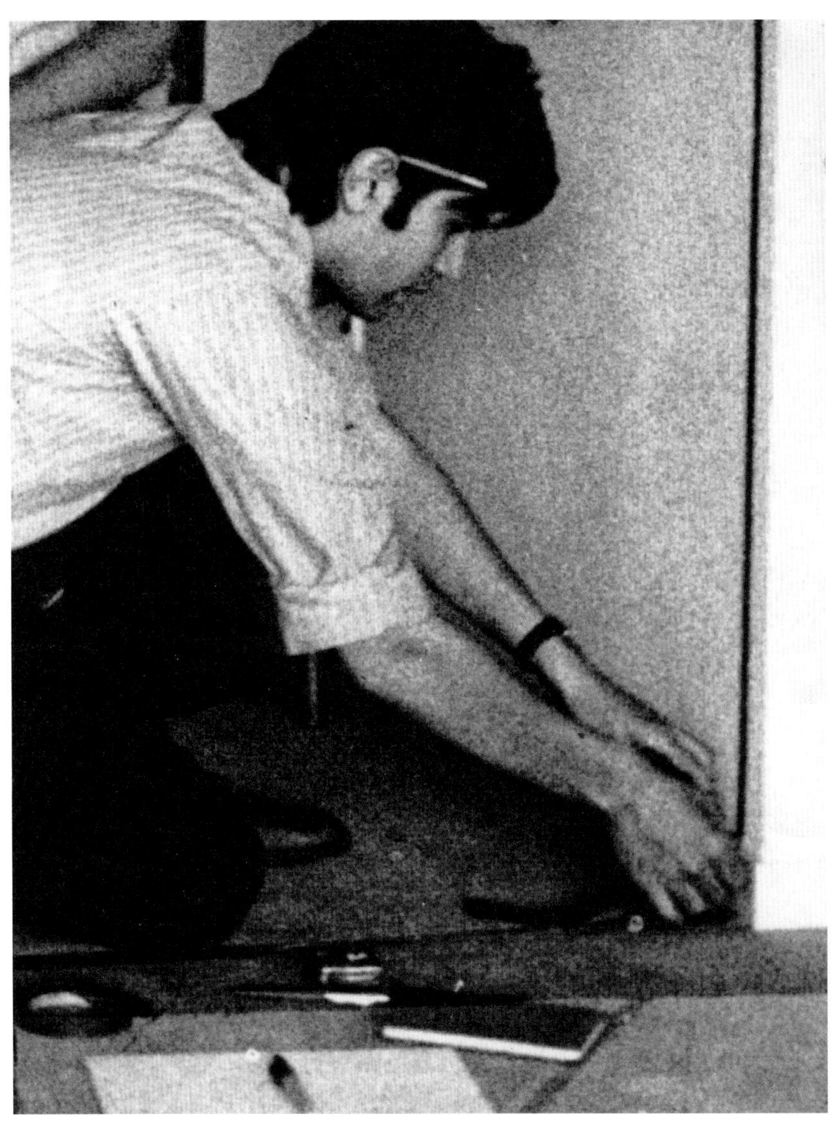

Mel Bochner installing *Measurement: Room*,
Galerie Heiner Friedrich, Munich, June 1969

Mel Bochner

Measurements (1968–1971)

Dia Art Foundation

Contents

Preface

Since its inception, Dia Art Foundation has helped artists experiment with systems, processes, and pure form that complicate our understanding of the world. One of the earliest Conceptual artists, Mel Bochner has exemplified such exploration over his five-decade career, deploying language and numbers as both concept and material, among other concerns, and working in a variety of media from prints, photographs, and paintings to large-scale installations. His Measurement series, the subject of this publication, uses a quotidian, empirical exercise to induce a phenomenological experience of space and subjectivity.

Published on the occasion of the fiftieth anniversary of his *Measurement: Room*, installed in 1969 at Galerie Heiner Friedrich in Munich, this volume and the exhibition it accompanies considers the genealogy of the work and Dia's history with Bochner. Designed by the artist with Phil Kovacevich, independent designer, and James Powers of Mel Bochner's studio, the publication tells the story of this remarkable series through working drawings, images of other Measurement works, and archival photographs of its historic first presentations, all complemented by new photography of the most recent iteration in this series installed at Dia Beacon, Beacon, New York. Heiner Friedrich's gallery, like Dia (the foundation he later cofounded with Philippa de Menil and Helen Winkler), was established as a haven for radical ideas that challenged the very notion of what an artwork could be. Bochner's *Measurement: Room*, which transforms the architectural envelope and the viewer's experience of this space into both subject and object of the work, epitomizes the bold gestures that Dia continues to cultivate. This blend of the archival and the new also guides the text contributions to the book. We are delighted to reprint a 1969 interview with Bochner about the series by the late Elayne Varian, a renowned art historian who served as an interlocutor for the artist throughout the 1960s and 1970s. As a counterpoint, in her essay, Alexis Lowry, curator at Dia, highlights the historical context of this series and its canny examination of indexical mapping, perception, and other spatial processes that structure our world.

We extend our deepest thanks to Mel Bochner. His thorough involvement with all aspects of the publication and exhibition enables Dia to do what it does best: collaborate with artists to advance their goals and inspire our visitors. Powers provided essential archival and technical support with the early phases of this project while, for the publication, Kovacevich added subtle enhancements to the original design and brought great care to the photographic reproductions.

We also owe a debt of gratitude to the individuals and institutions whose financial backing helped realize this endeavor. This exhibition is made possible by generous support from the Ampersand Foundation. Additional support is provided by Jill and Peter Kraus, Simon Lee, and Susan and Larry Marx. Support for the publication is provided by Lisa and Tom Blumenthal; Peter Freeman, Inc.; Evelyn and David Lasry/Two Palms, New York; and Marc Selwyn Fine Art.

James Meyer, curatorial and academic advisor, brought this project to Dia and enthusiastically advocated for a reprisal and expansion of Bochner's pioneering vision. Lowry also championed this exhibition and publication and saw them to fruition. In Development, Karey David, director of development and foundation and government relations; Kseniya Ignatova-Yates, manager, major giving and campaign; and David Morehouse, deputy director of advancement, raised crucial support for both the publication and exhibition. Heidie Giannotti, director of exhibition design and installation, and the team at Atomic Signs, New York, were essential to the installation in Beacon. Maria Celi, director of visitor experience; Caroline Schneider, visitor services manager; Daniel Oates-Kuhn, visitor services assistant manager; and Colleen Kinneary-McCabe, bookshop manager, welcomed our visitors to the galleries. Kamilah N. Foreman, director of publications; Mollie Bernstein, rights and reproductions associate; Sophia Larigakis, editorial and publications assistant; and Elizabeth Franzen, independent editor, skillfully maintained the artist's vision in producing the book. The ever-reliable Bill Jacobson of Bill Jacobson Studio created the stunning photographs of the exhibition.

To measure is to assess, to locate oneself and one's environment, and this semicentennial installation is an important measure of Dia and its fidelity to artists and to its mission.

Jessica Morgan
Nathalie de Gunzburg Director
Dia Art Foundation

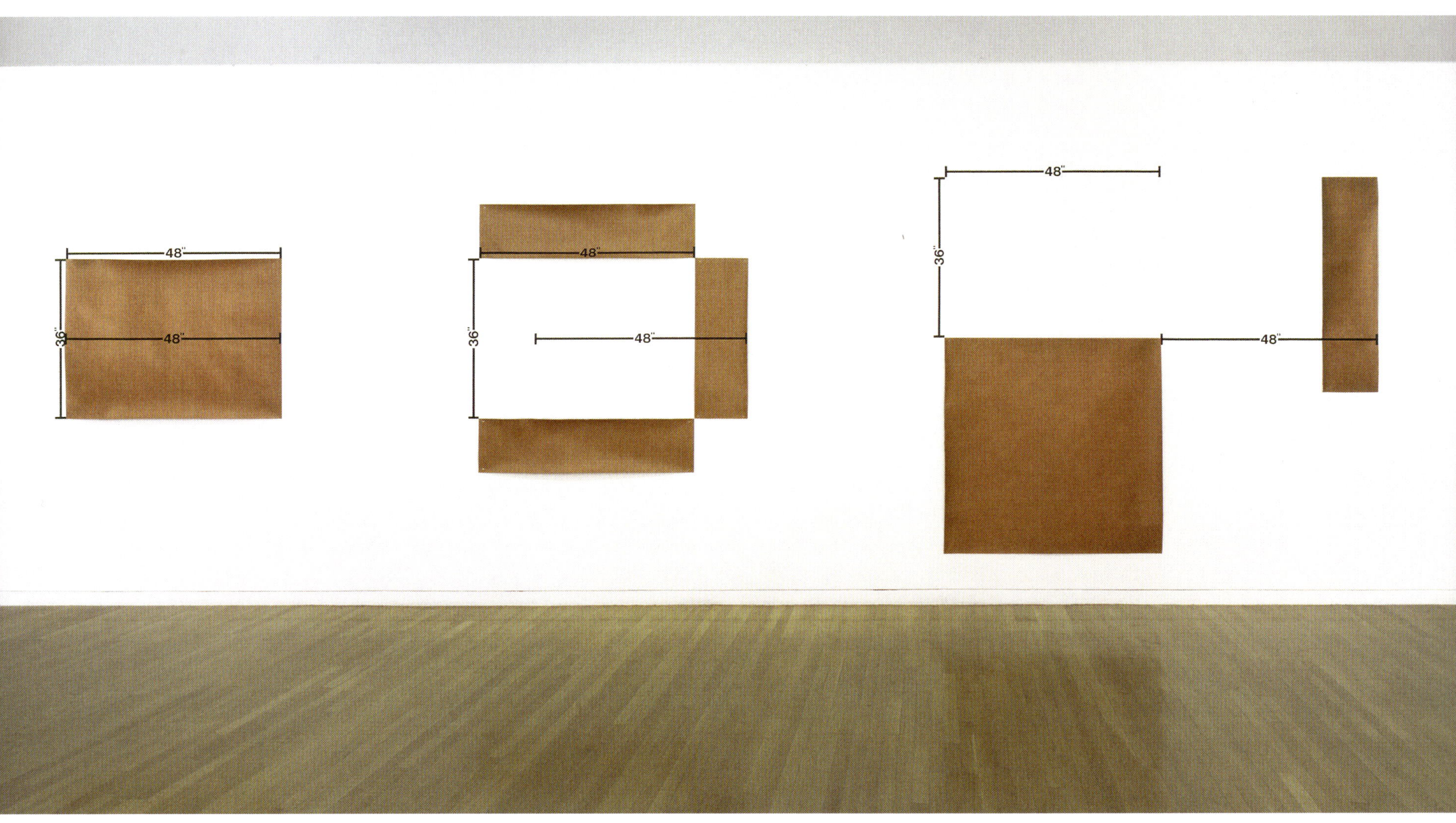

48 Inches Standards: Set A, 1969
Letraset and brown paper on wall, three parts
96 × 300 inches overall
Solomon R. Guggenheim Museum, New York, Purchased with funds contributed by the Collections Council
Installation view, *As Painting, Division and Displacement*, Wexner Center for the Arts, Columbus, Ohio, 2001

Elayne Varian: Let's talk about your Measurement works. What is the idea behind them?

Mel Bochner: It seems to me that our perception of things is determined by the ideas that we have about them. It's a case of a certain mental space that one has for both seeing and thinking. We like to feel that they are separate, but they are not—they overlap. They overlap in our conception of things, and consequently, our experience of them.

EV: Are you talking about art?

MB: I am talking about human activity and art as an activity of the mind. For me art is a way of thinking about things. By superimposing the measurements of a thing on the thing itself, I incorporate it into my art. This happens because it forces you to locate the space in the mind where one both thinks about and sees an object. It's a question of containment.

EV: Why did you choose to work with brown paper?

MB: The brown paper began as just a convenience, something that was always around the studio. It came in sizes, three feet by four feet, which are the standard measurements of most building materials. I slowly came to realize that these measurements are so deeply embedded in our experience that they regulate our perception, yet remain completely invisible. That's how 36 inches and 48 inches became the givens in the 48" Standard pieces. Brown paper itself had no aesthetic interest to me as a material, but as I began working with it I found that it had its own very interesting properties. For instance, I found that wrapping paper not only comes in standard sizes but in standard weights: sixty-pound papers, eighty-pound papers, ninety-pound papers. I made a couple of pieces that look exactly alike but differ imperceptibly because one comes from a sixty-pound roll and the other from a ninety-pound roll. Also, the paper's materiality led me to other ways of thinking with it . . . the way it folds, the way it wrinkles, the way it crumples, the way it rolls and unrolls. What I've been trying to do is raise these processes to the level of thought.

EV: When you sell a piece, do you sell a drawing of the piece or a photograph?

MB: The person receives some evidence of ownership—a signed drawing or photograph—and, of course, the piece itself, which I make for them.

EV: Is this because you draw it directly on the wall?

MB: Yes.

EV: Does that mean it can never be in an exhibition because it only exists on that specific wall?

MB: On the contrary. The piece could be in my studio, and in someone's collection, and in an exhibition simultaneously. It doesn't come down in one place and go up in another. In this sense the piece is not a portable object, it's a portable idea. As long as the internal relationships of measurements and materials remain constant, it's the same work no matter where it is. Physical location is merely a minor variable. Other pieces I've been thinking about would make a specific physical location the constant and the material a variable, so that something would have to be in a certain place at a certain time . . .

EV: Before we began talking about materials, you said something about containment.

MB: The way things are contained physically and mentally is an important issue to me. For example, the measurements that are marked on the wall around the sheet of paper read *36" x 48"*. However, to measure the entire work you must include the two-inch width of the numbers, which makes the actual measurement of the piece 38 by 50 inches. In other words, in order to contain the boundaries you must inevitably enlarge them *ad infinitum*. I think that the real subject of these pieces is boundaries—the perceptual boundaries of thought. How much of something do we include within our field, how are the boundaries determined, how much of it is visible, how much of it is filled in by the viewer, how much of it doesn't need to be filled in—how much of it can exist without any physicality?

EV: I like your use of the word "container," because in your case it's the wall that's the container.

MB: Yes, but I also think of the "container" as a somewhat more ambiguous notion. What is the container, let's say, in *Thirteen Sheets of 8" Graph Paper (From a Nonfinite Series)*, the piece I did for the *When Attitude Becomes Form* exhibition? It's made up of thirteen sheets of standard eight-inch graph paper, with the width of each sheet drawn across it. The sheets are hung next to each other in a horizontal row by staples in the upper corners of each sheet. As the show travels, I ask them to pull them down, tearing a part of the corner off, so that one measurement of the sheet, the unmarked vertical measurement, will decrease constantly at an unknown rate. If the exhibition travels long enough, the work might finally disappear completely, except for little bits of it tacked to walls in all the different museums where the show has been.

EV: Well, how do you refer to your work, as painting or sculpture?

MB: I try not to refer to it as either.

EV: I think of the *Measurements* as "volumes," but I can't think of them as sculpture.

MB: I like that because the *Measurement: Room*, where I mark the measurements of a room directly on the walls like a three-dimensional blueprint, encompasses a concept of volume, without becoming a sculpture. Rather than think about my work categorically as painting or sculpture, I think of it more like gerunds, verbs that act like nouns. So that the work is an active thing, both the doing and the thing done. It could be a simple question of orientation, like placing something in a specific position, for example, in relation to the compass. I feel that the basic question in my work—back to containment again—is how do you experience yourself in the world, which is to say, how do you inhabit an *idea* of the world?

EV: Does your work have an architectural basis?

MB: Well, only in the general sense that my work uses architecture as a support. But it's not about the specifics of a place. In other words, my work is not about the phenomenology of architecture. What I'm trying to do is look critically at how experience is formed and to question the weight of that experience. One of the reasons that the means I use are so ephemeral, so "thin," is to undermine the domination of architecture, force it to surrender its transparency.

EV: To me these recent works have a kind of illusion that nothing else you've done before has.

MB: There is one piece that I want to do [*No Vantage Point: Eye Level Cross-Section of a Room*], 1969, which may be even more illusory, because I think it might transform the literal itself into an illusion. I want to draw a line on the wall all around the room at my eye level. My "horizon line." Horizon is a powerful metaphor in our culture for so many kinds of ideas and experiences. In any room which one occupies, such as my studio or your office, you establish your presence as a line of sight. Everything above and below is then subconsciously related to that imaginary horizontal cross-section. My piece will force you to become aware of your own eye level as a physical boundary, the literal plateau from which you see the world. My intention is to change the work of art's function for the viewer. Art would go from being the record of someone else's perception to becoming the recognition of your own.

EV: But isn't that like saying that walking down the street and seeing something beautiful can be an aesthetic experience? That doesn't make it a work of art, does it?

MB: I'm not sure what makes anything a work of art. What I'm trying to do is test the limits of the definitions. I can think of three categories of things. There is the large category of natural things, things without pre-definition. Rocks, trees, and people are facts of nature, they exist before they are defined. A second category would be artificial but useful things, like a hammer or a tape recorder, things we make to apply our will to the world. The third category would be works of art, artificial but "use-less." If you look at things from this perspective there is no categorical imperative for what a work of art should be . . . or, for that matter, what it could be.

EV: But then how do you know it is a work of art? Couldn't the viewer just pass it by?

MB: Yes, they could. But that's OK. Those who pass it by, pass it by. My interest is in focusing down on a finer and keener realization of what things are in themselves. That means the calming and quieting of the personality of the work. I'm not trying to highlight an "experience." I just want to make it available without fanfare, without drama. What you decide to do with it is up to you.

Elayne Varian (1913–1987) was director of the Finch College Museum of Art, New York.

8½ × 11 Inches, 1968

Typewritten text on paper

11 × 8½ inches

8½" x 11"

Opposite

Singer Notes, 1968

Ink on graph paper, sheet 43

11 × 8½ inches

Following pages

Singer Notes, 1968

Typewritten text on paper, sheets 45–46

11 × 8½ inches

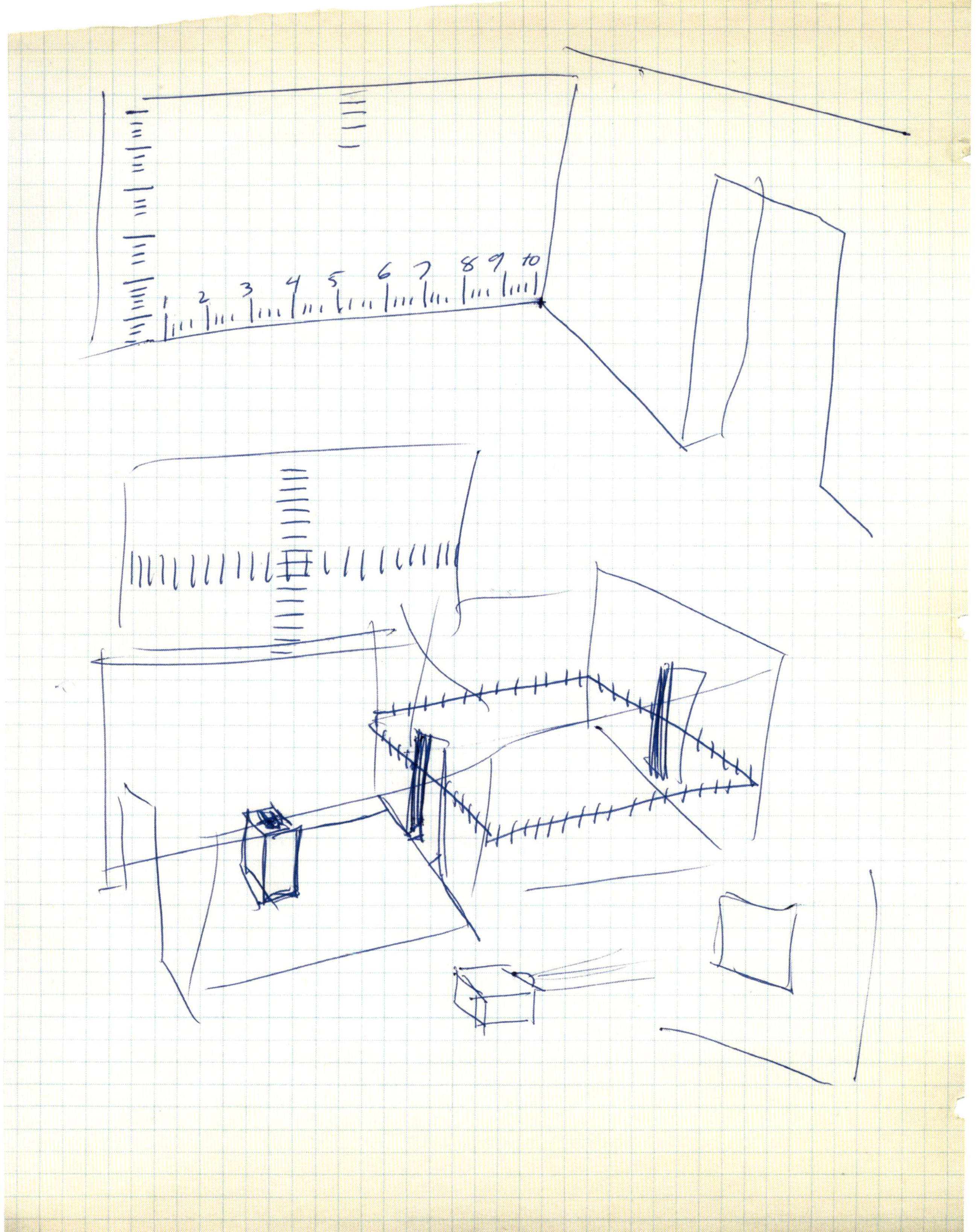
1 2 3 4 5 6 7 8 9 10

LEFT WALL HEIGHT NINETY-SIX INCHES

LEFT WALL LENGTH ONE HUNDRED AND FOUR INCHES

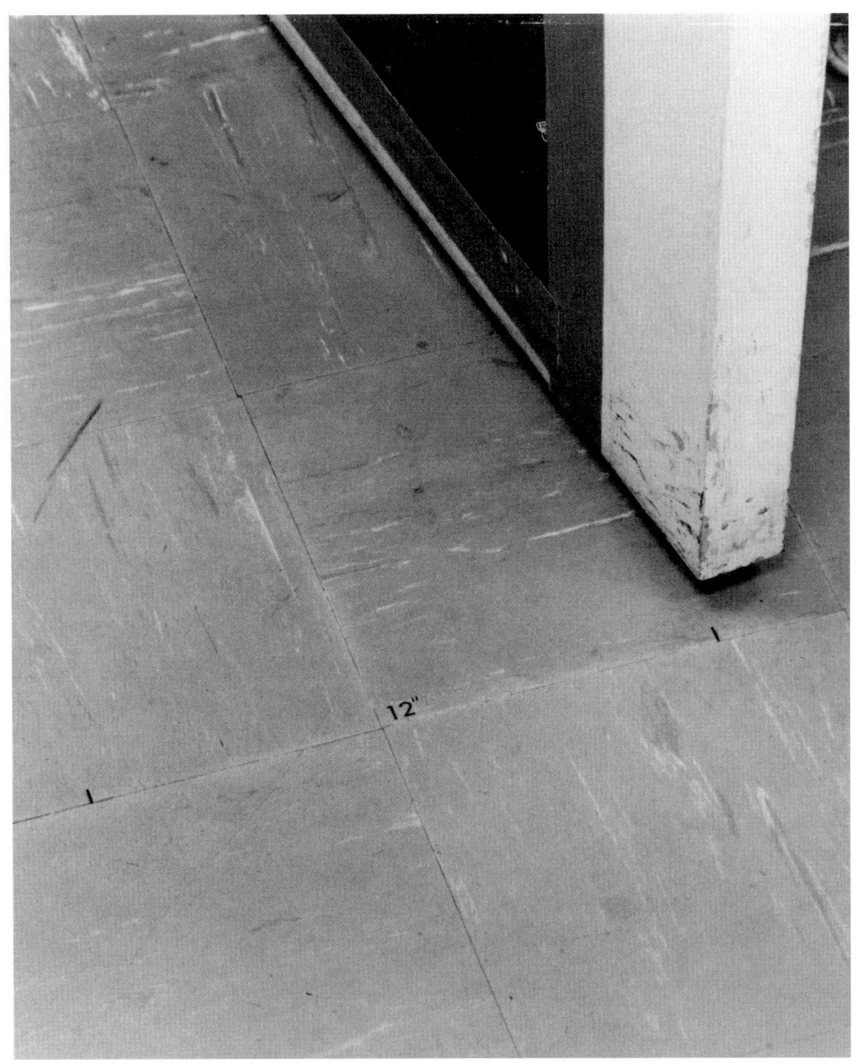

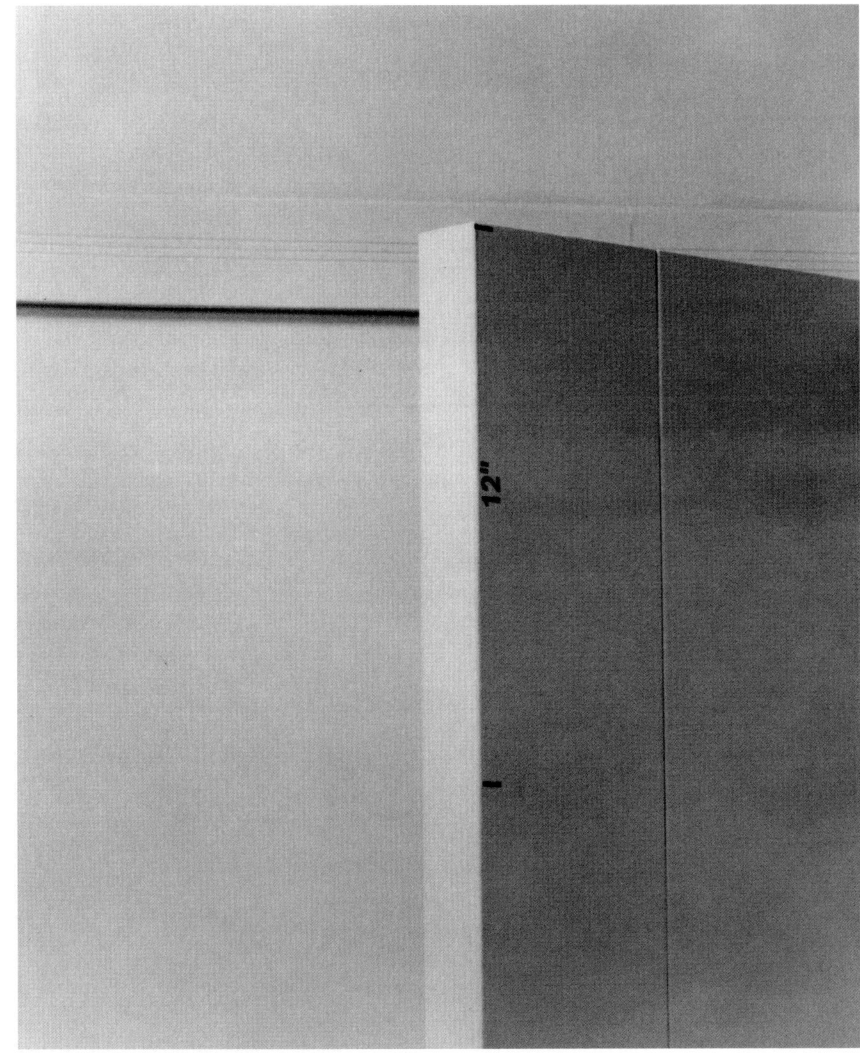

Singer Lab Measurements, 1968

Gelatin silver prints, nos. 1–4

10 × 8 inches each

Installation views, Singer Laboratories, Denville, New Jersey

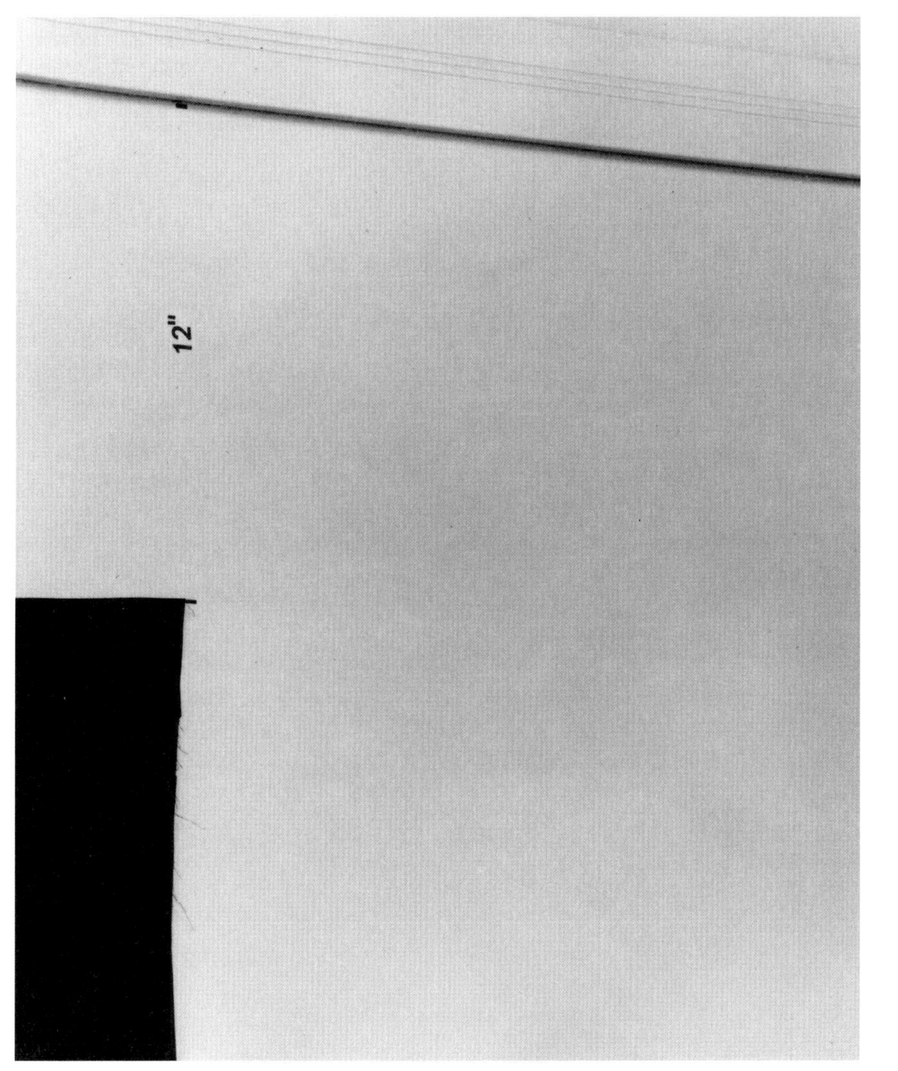
12"

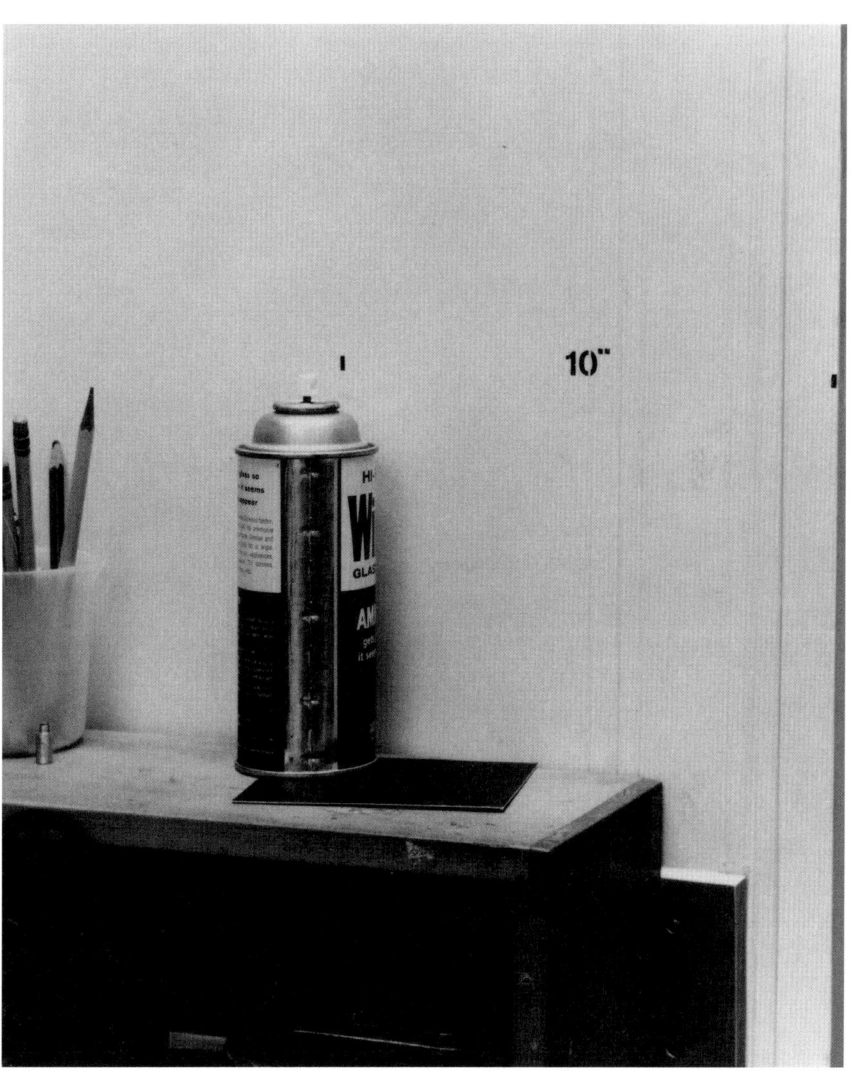
10"

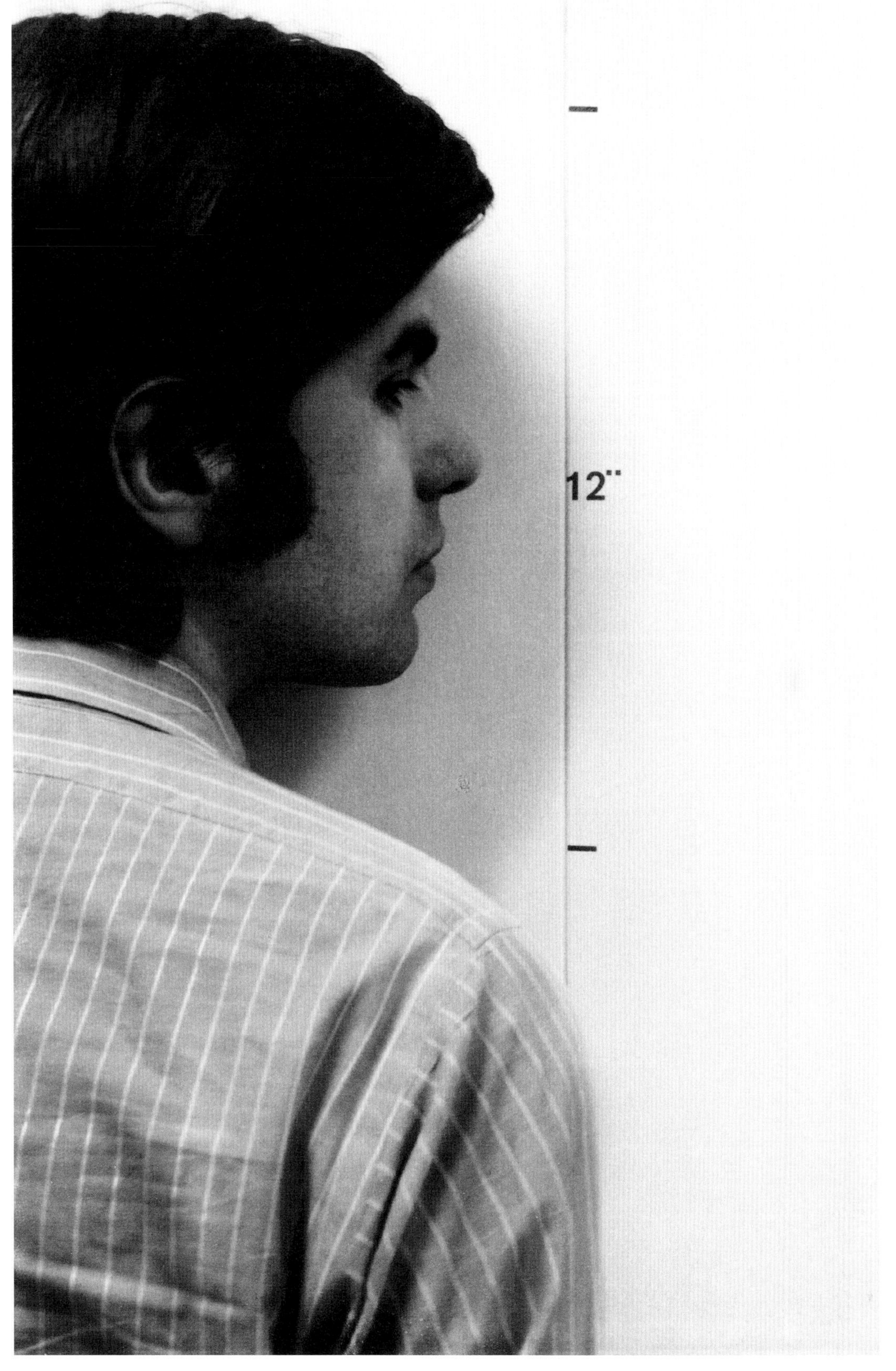
12"

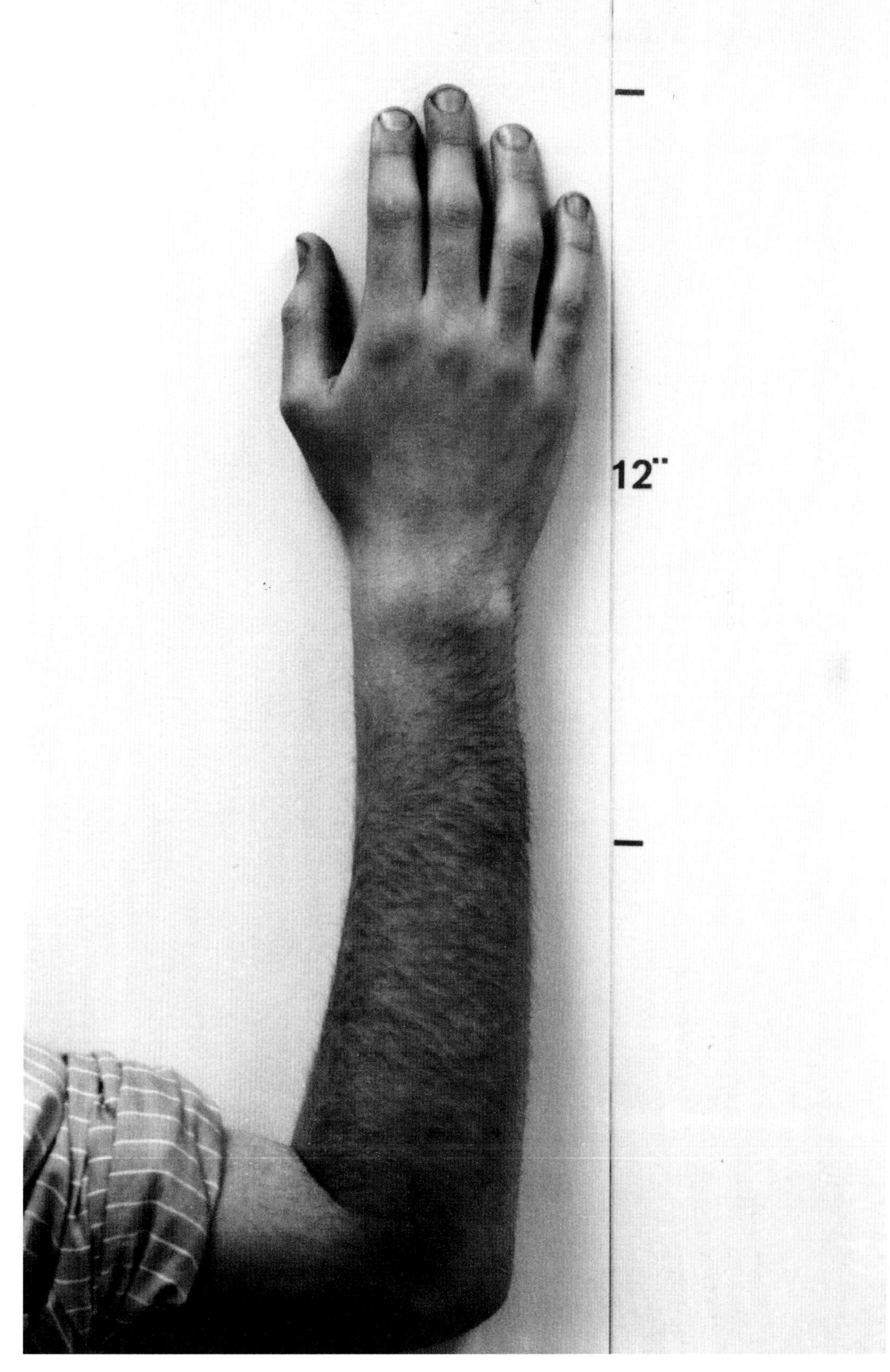
12"

Previous pages

Actual Size: (Face and Hand), 1968

Gelatin silver prints

22 × 14¼ inches each

Measurement: 90 Degrees (Fold), 1969

Ink on paper

11 × 17 inches

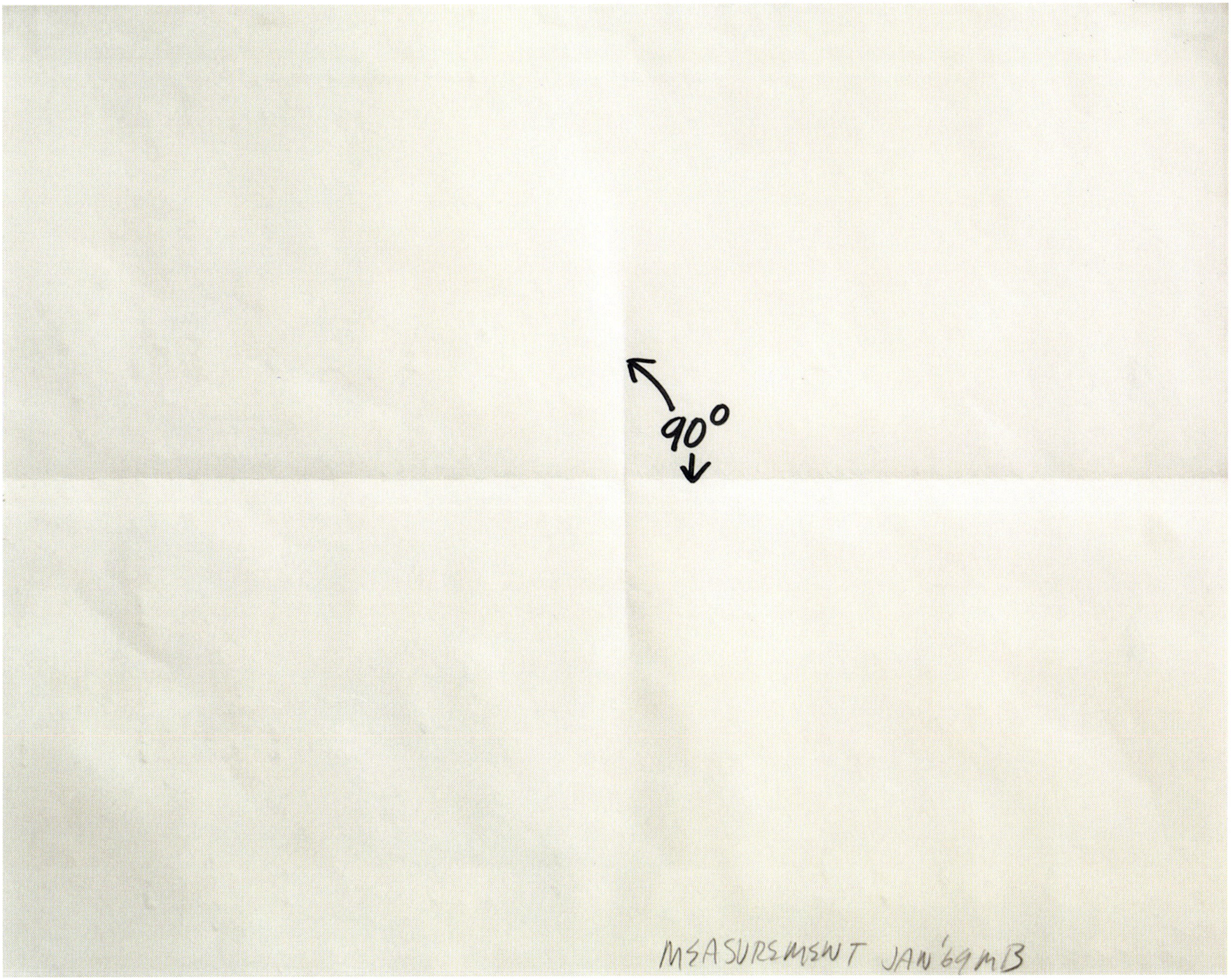

90°

MEASUREMENT JAN '69 MB

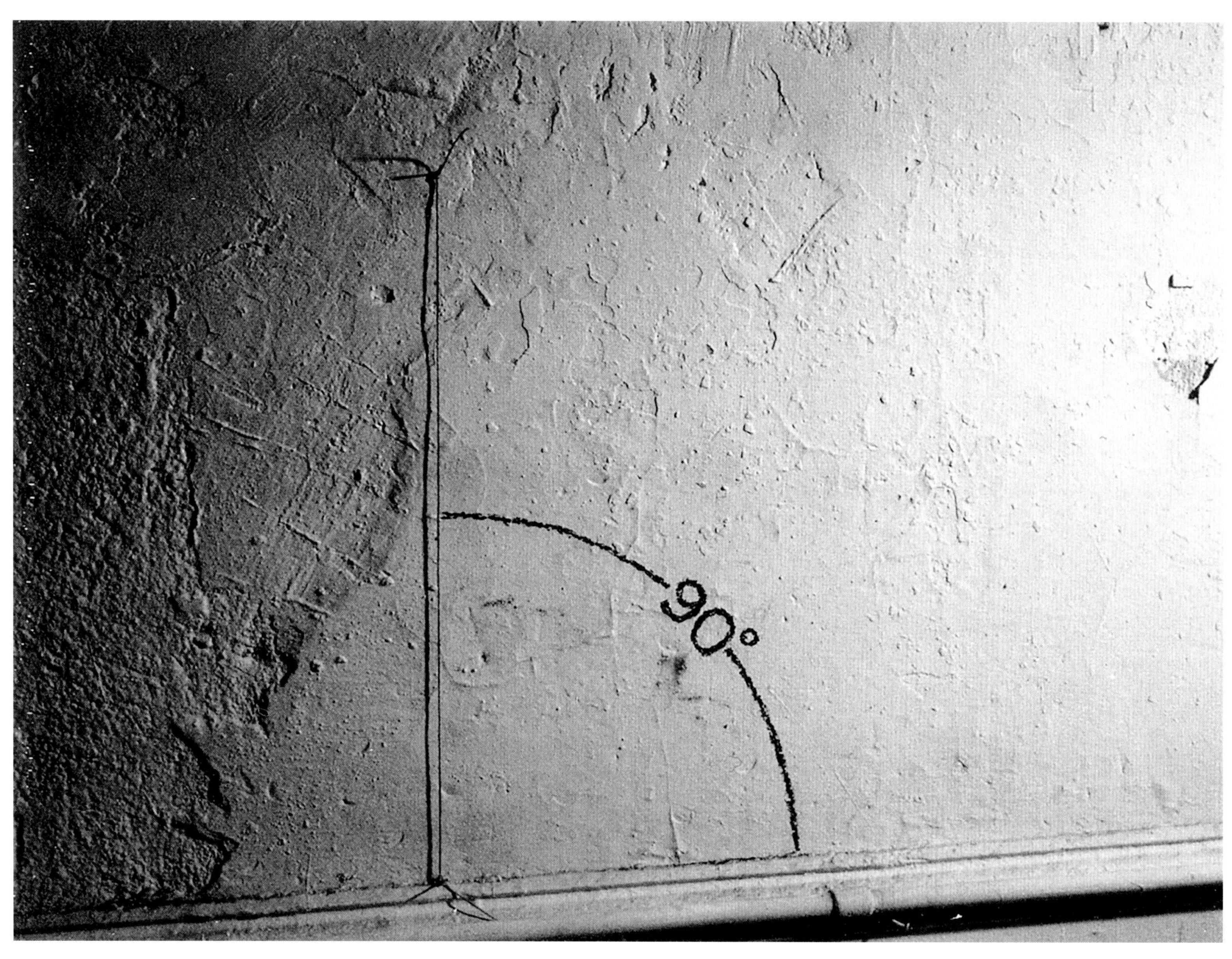

Measurement: 90 Degrees, 1968

Twine, nails, and charcoal on wall

Installation view, artist's studio, New York

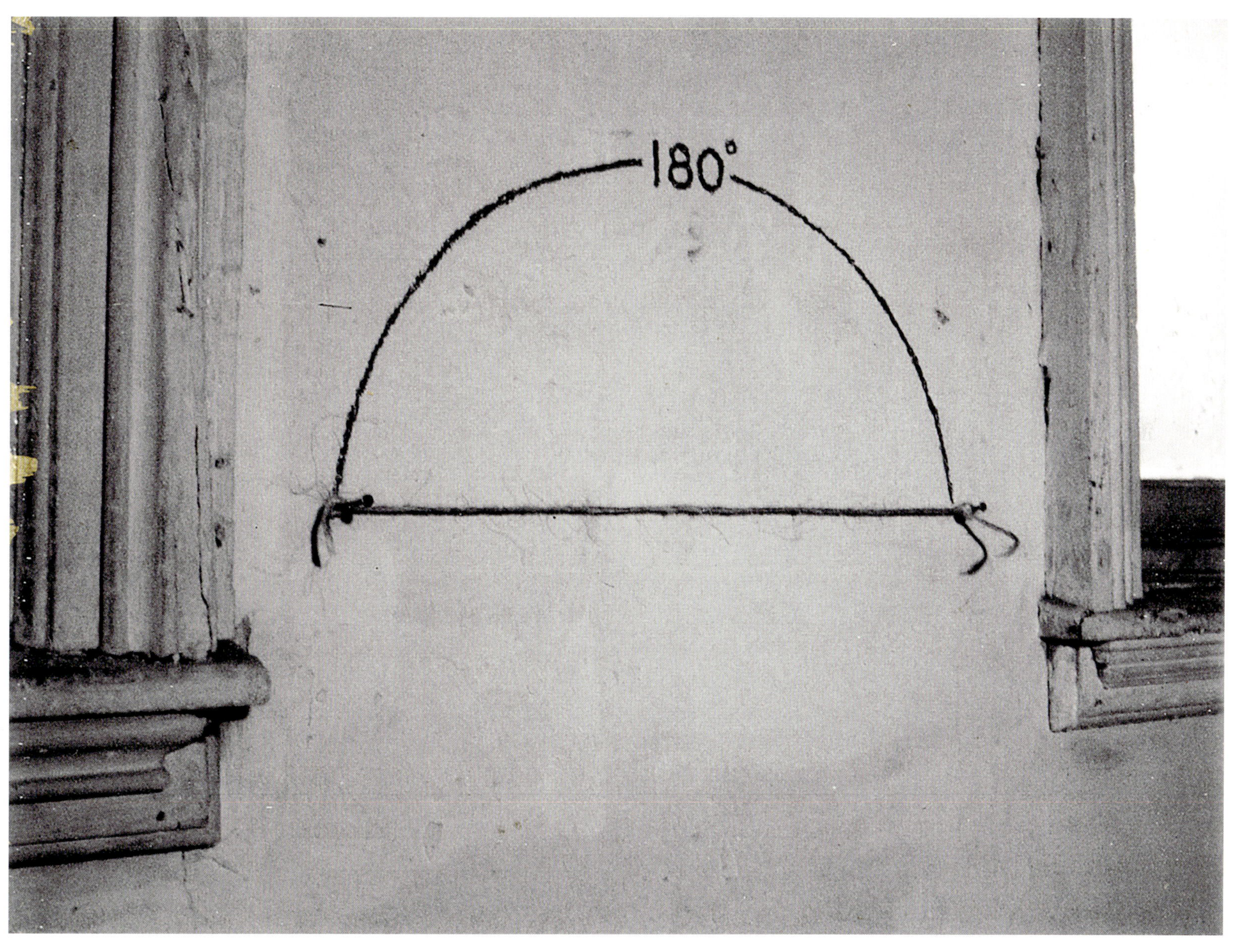

Measurement: 180 Degrees, 1968

Twine, nails, and charcoal on wall

Installation view, artist's studio, New York

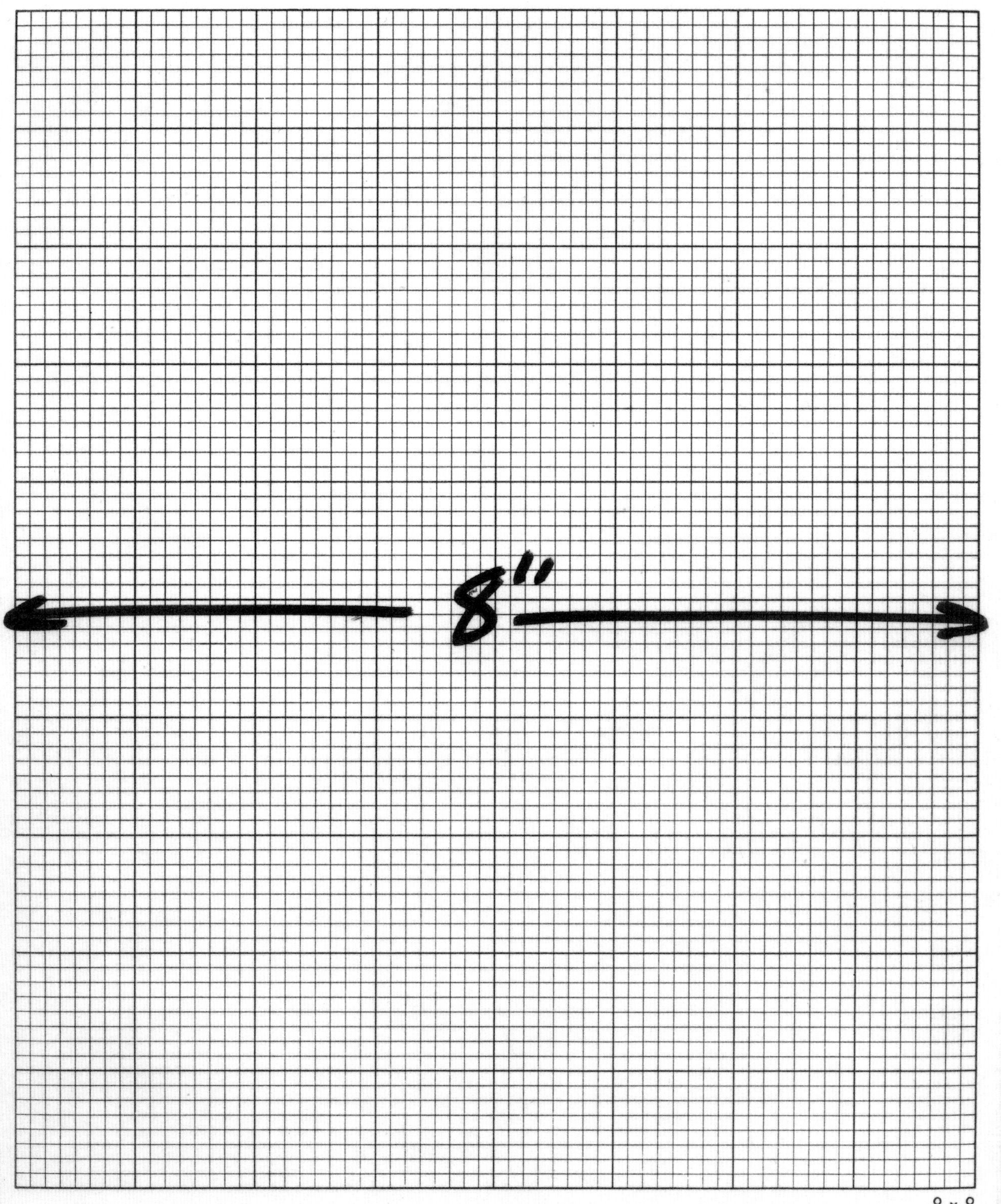
8"
8 x 8
MEL BOCHNER 1969

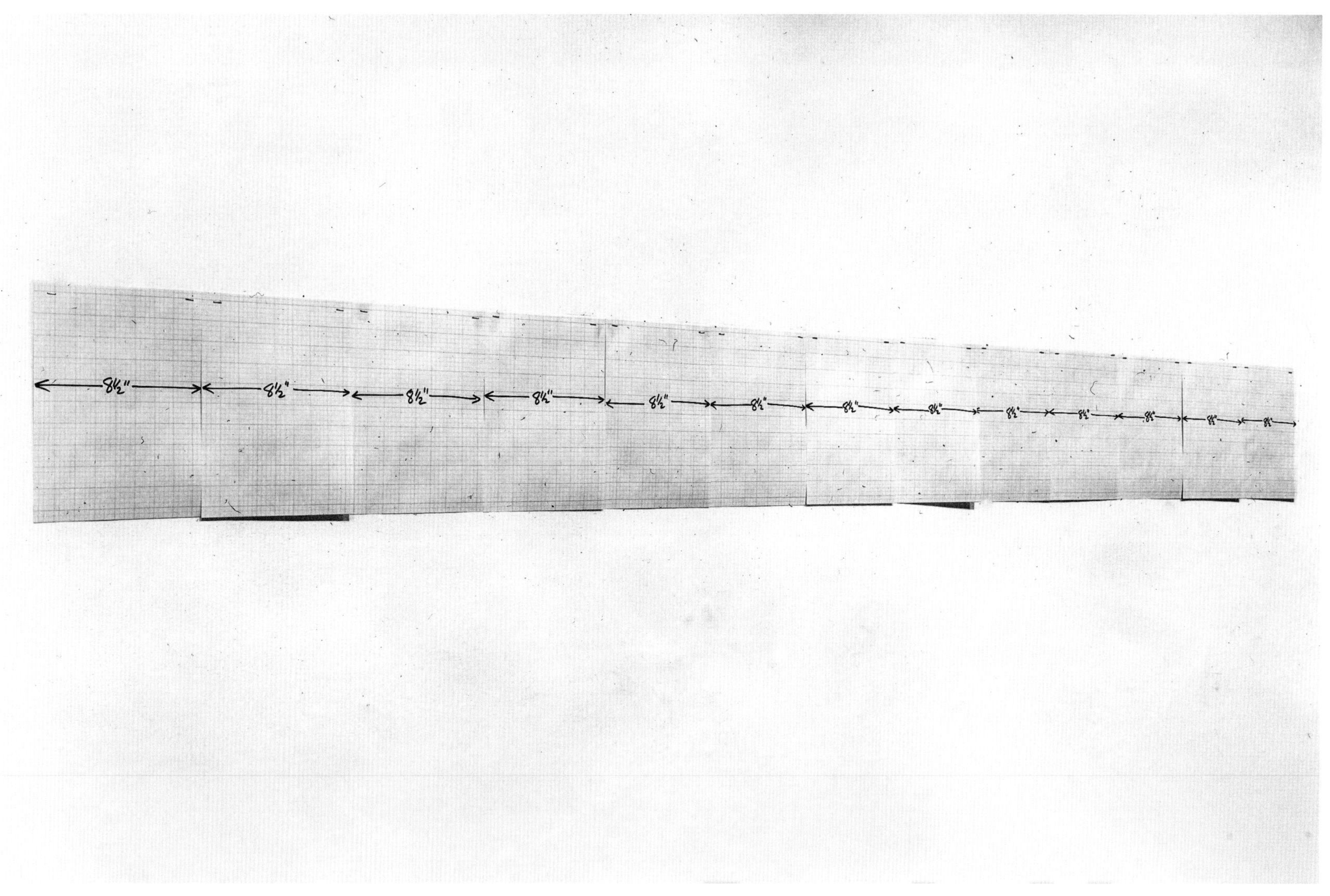

8 Inch Measurement, 1969

Pen on graph paper

11 × 8½ inches

Art Institute of Chicago, Gift of Irving Stenn Jr.

13 Sheets of 8½ Inch Graph Paper (from a Nonfinite Series), 1968

Ink on graph paper stapled to wall, 13 parts

11 × 110½ inches overall

Installation view, *When Attitude Becomes Form*, Kunsthalle Bern, Switzerland, 1969

17 Inch Measurement, 1969

Ink on graph paper

14 × 17 inches

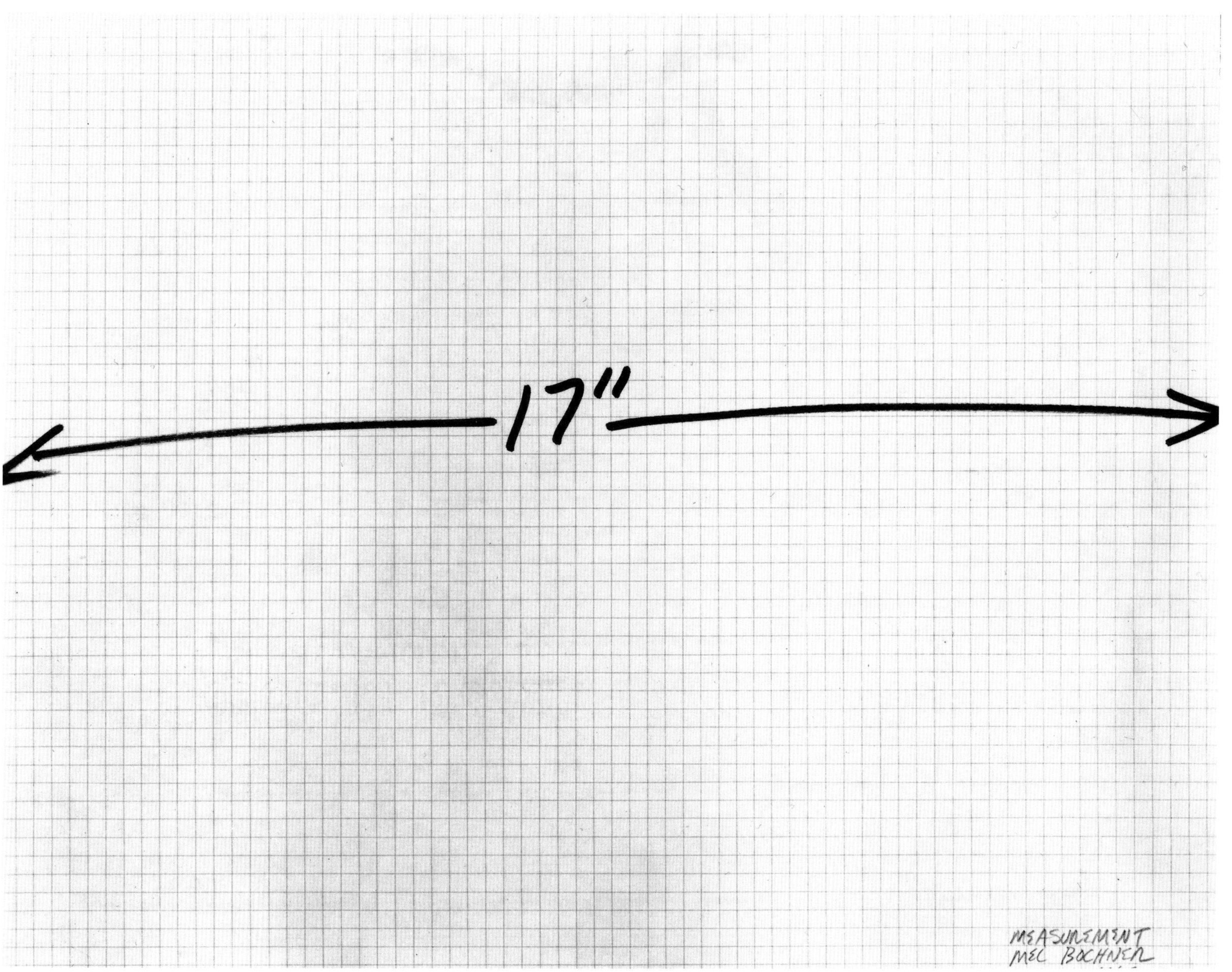
17"
MEASUREMENT
MEL BOCHNER

48 Inch Standards (#1), 1969

Letraset, tape, and brown paper stapled to wall

38 × 50 inches

Collection of Suzanne F. Cohen, Baltimore

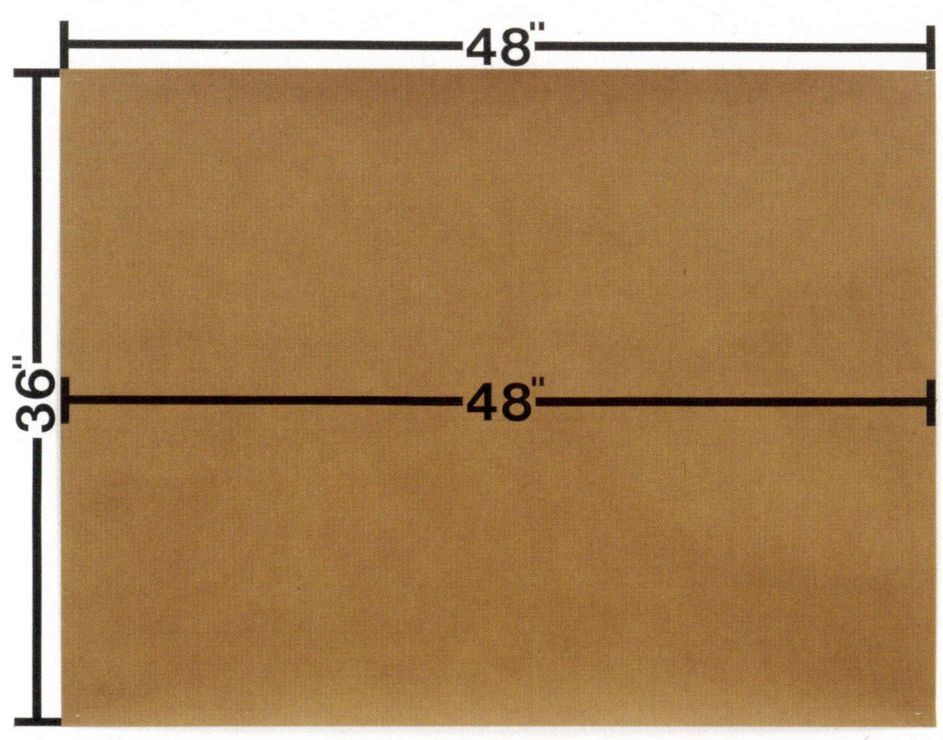
48"
36"
48"

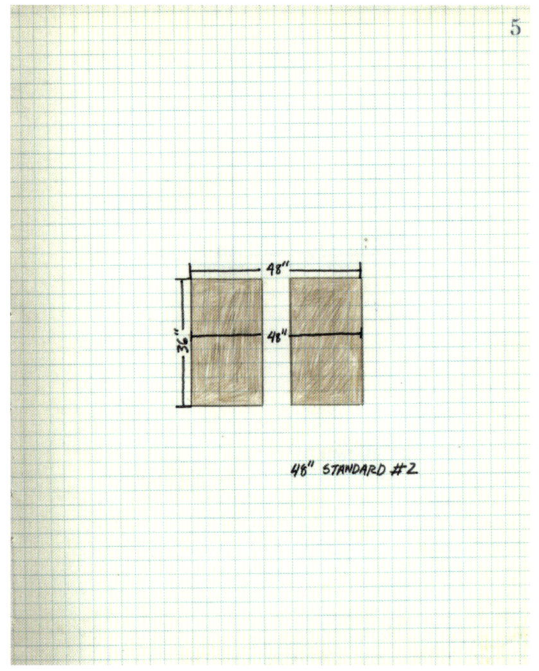

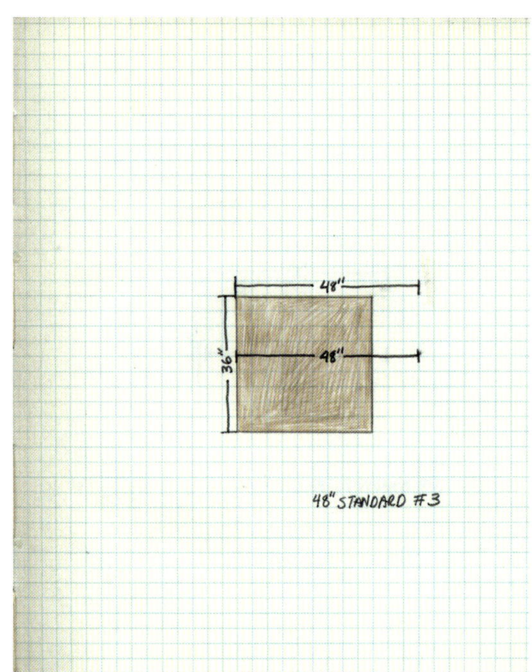

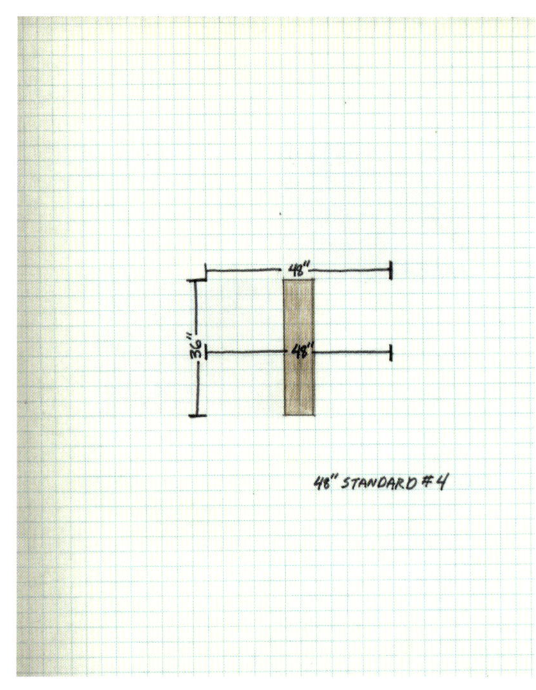

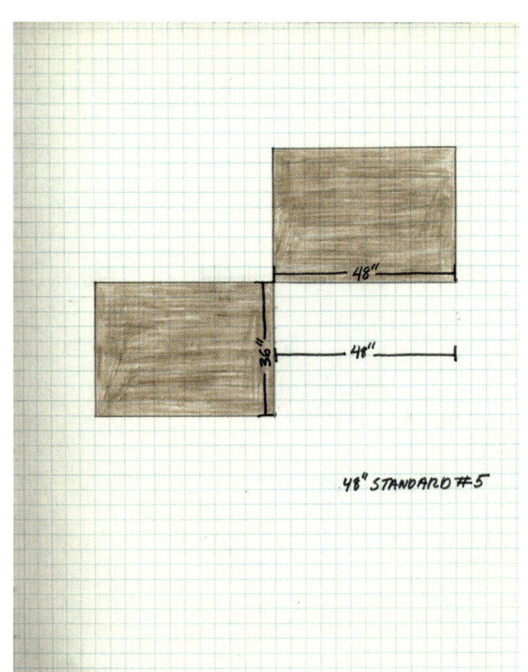

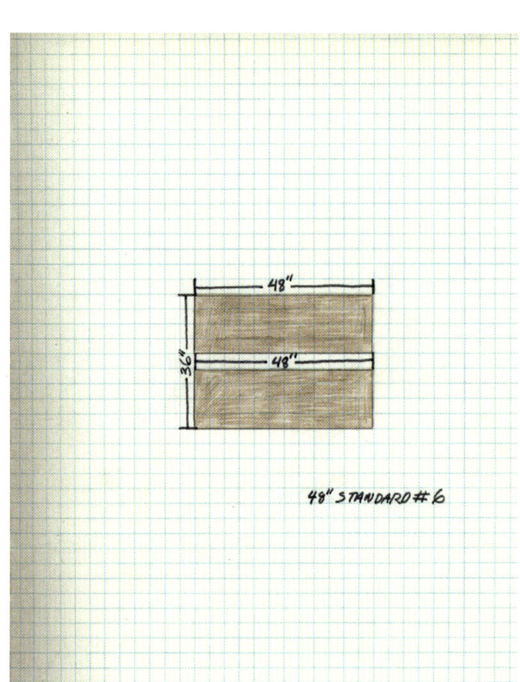

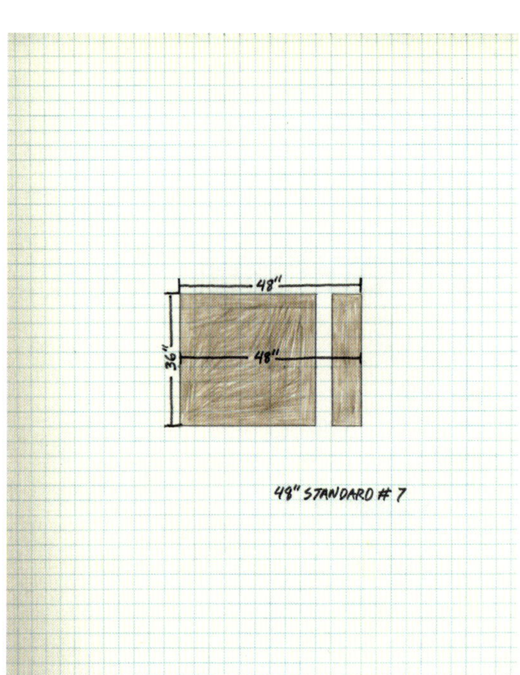

48 Inch Standards Notebook, 1969

Pencil and pen on notebook paper, 12 of 28 sheets

10 × 7¾ inches each

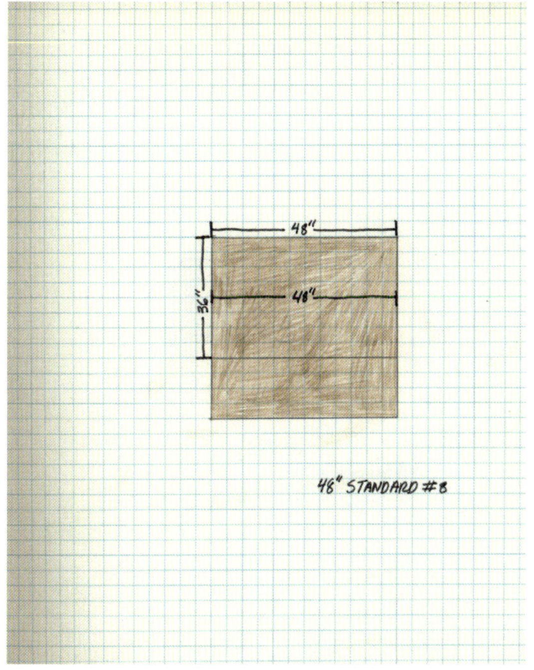
48"
48"
36"
48" STANDARD #8

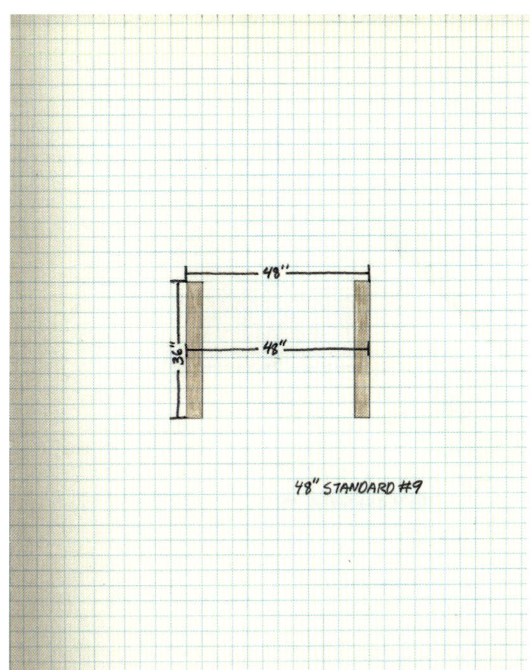
48"
48"
36"
48" STANDARD #9

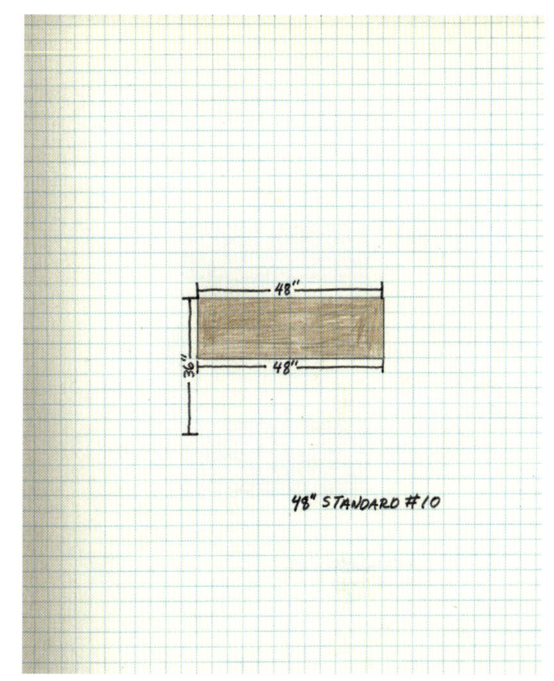
48"
48"
36"
48" STANDARD #10

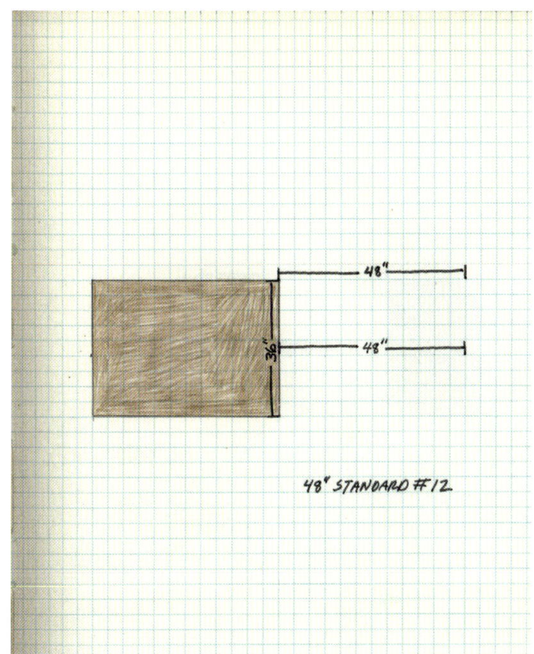
48"
48"
36"
48" STANDARD #12

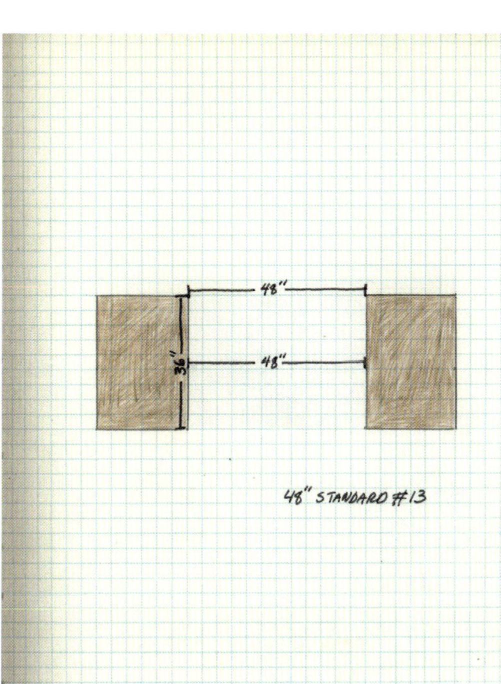
48"
48"
36"
48" STANDARD #13

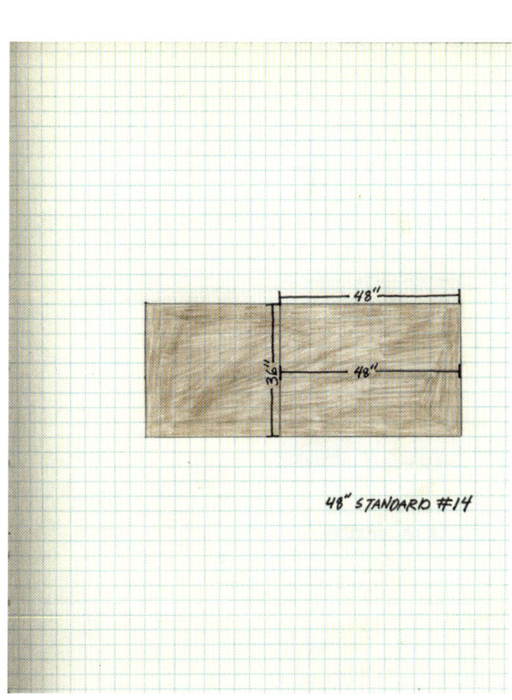
48"
48"
36"
48" STANDARD #14

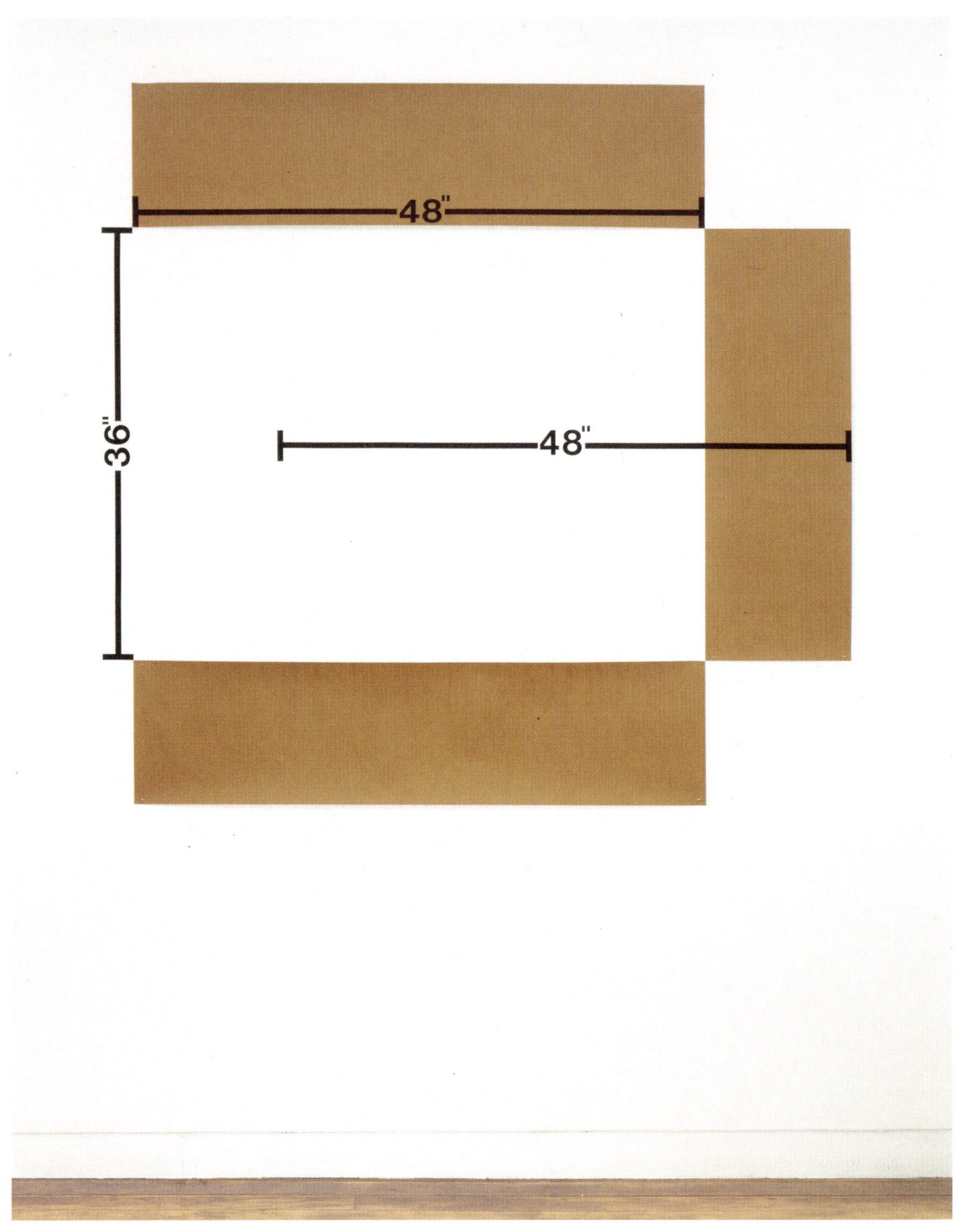

48 Inch Standards (#11), 1969

Letraset, tape, and brown paper stapled to wall

60 × 62 inches

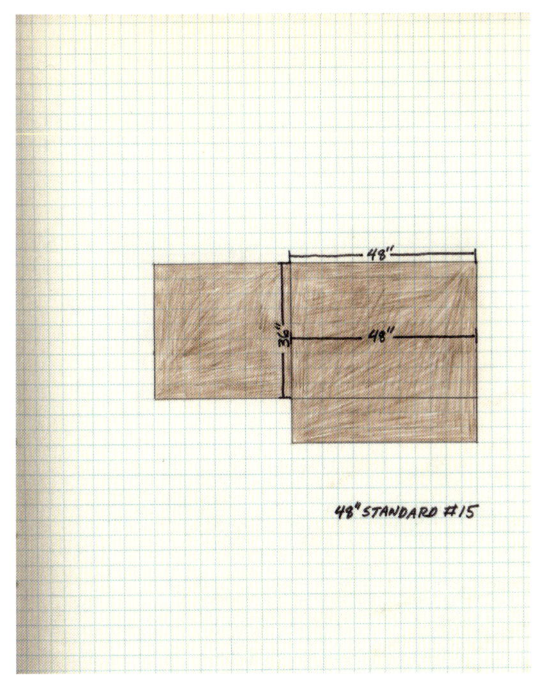

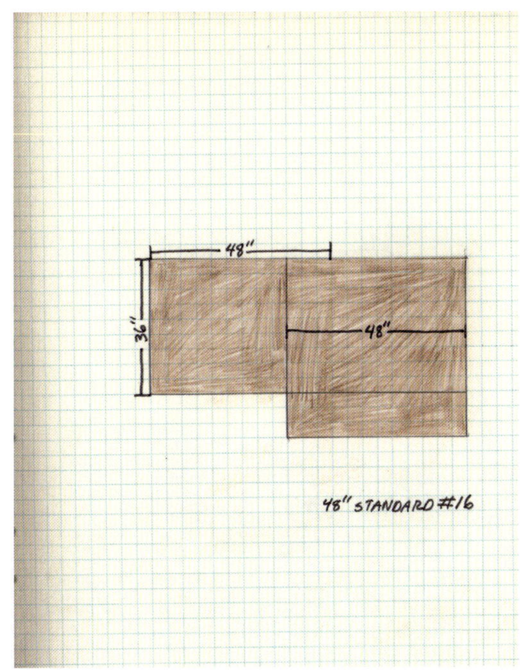

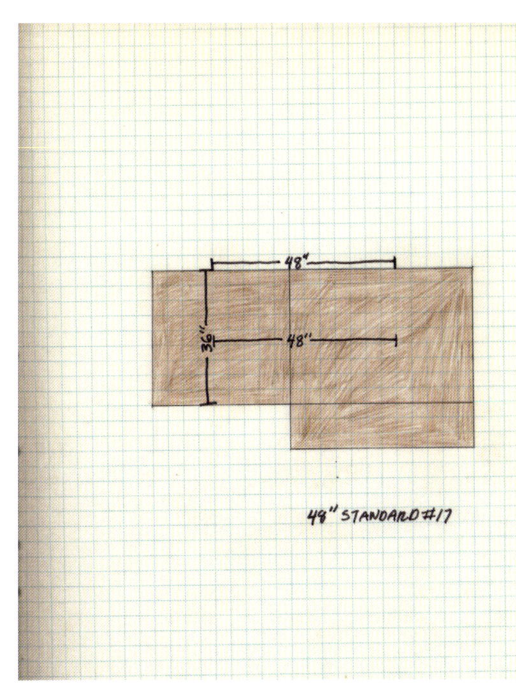

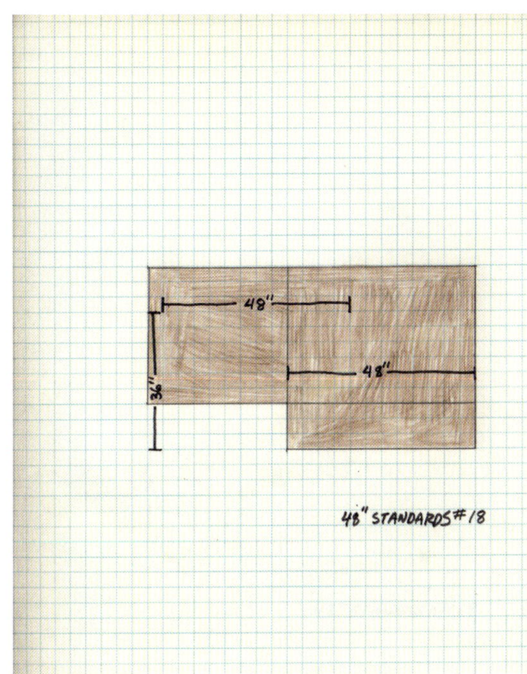

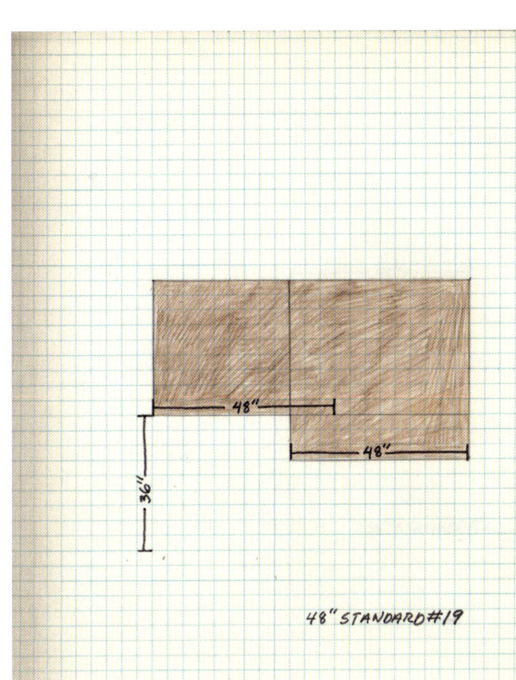

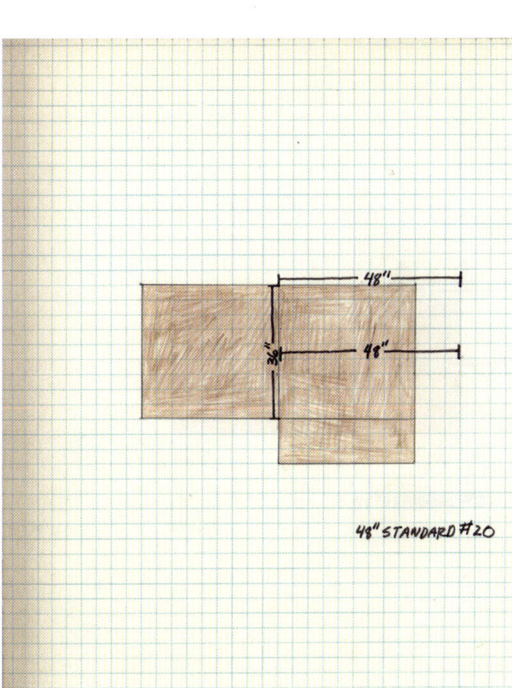

48 Inch Standards Notebook, 1969

Pencil and pen on notebook paper, 6 of 28 sheets

10 × 7¾ inches each

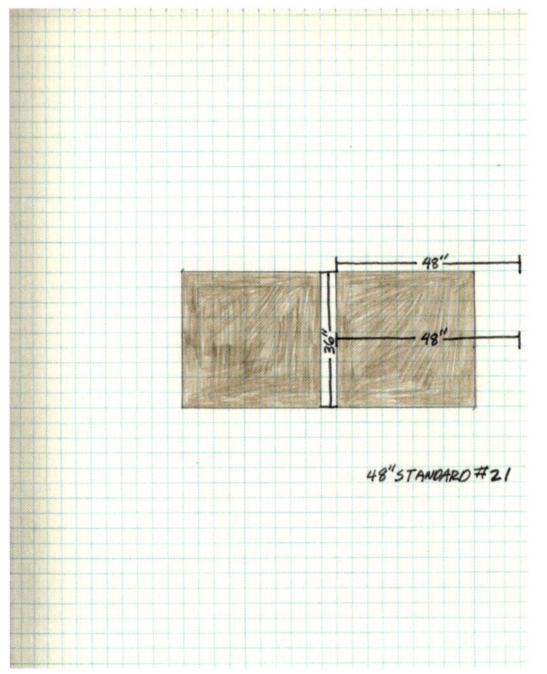

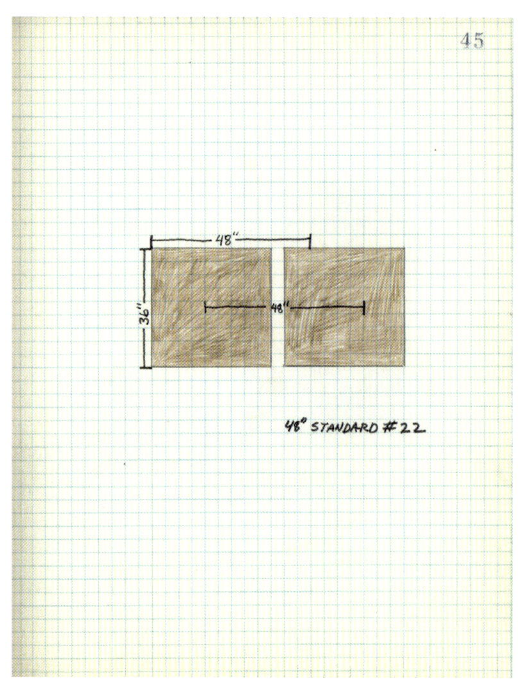

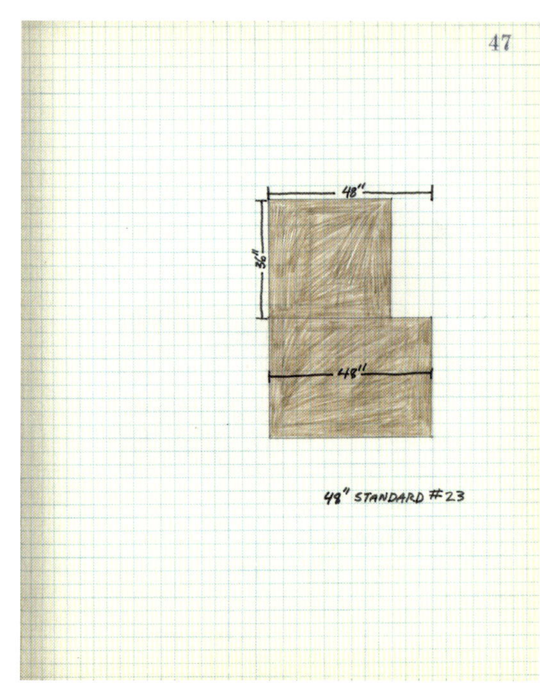

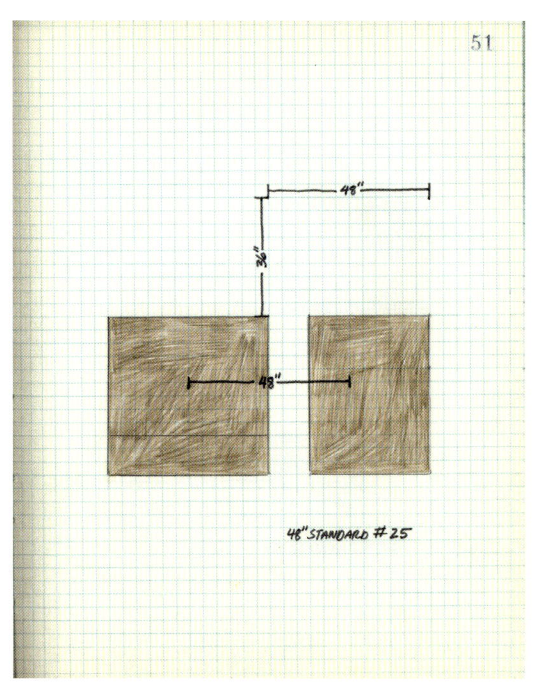

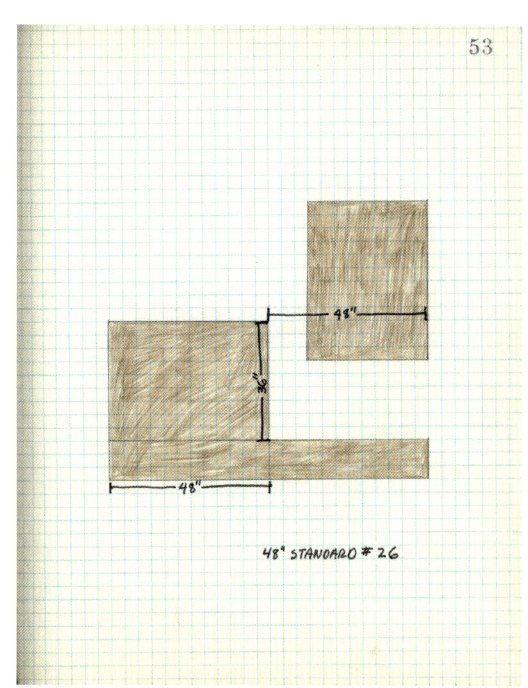

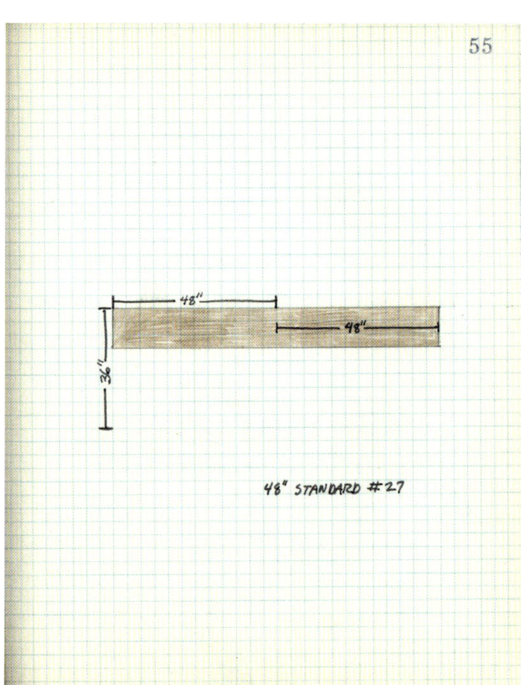

48 Inch Standards Notebook, 1969

Pencil and pen on notebook paper, 6 of 28 sheets

10 × 7¾ inches each

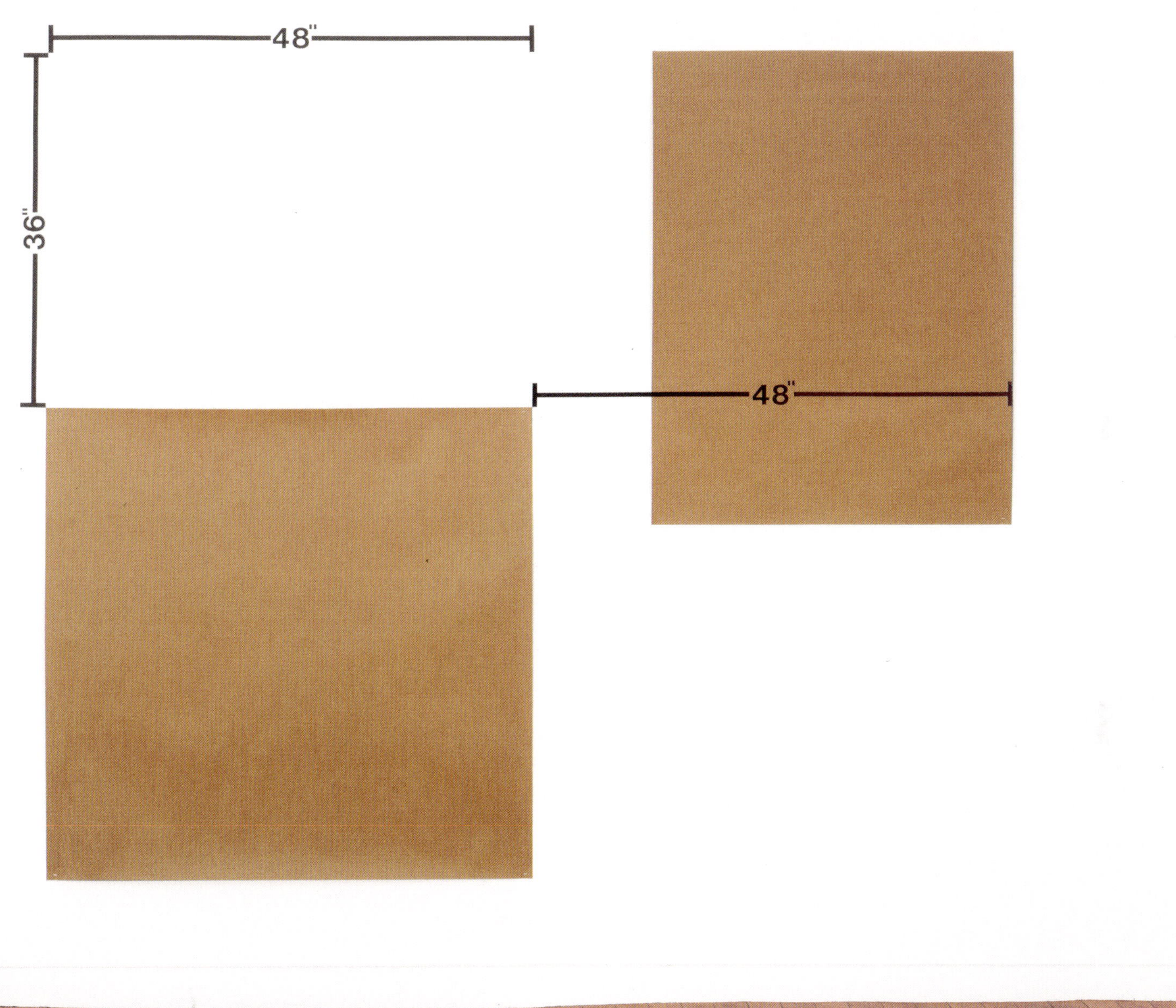

48 Inch Standards (#24), 1969

Letraset, tape, and brown paper stapled to wall

86 × 98 inches

48 Inch Standards (#28a), 1969

Letraset, tape, and brown paper stapled to wall

86 × 146 inches

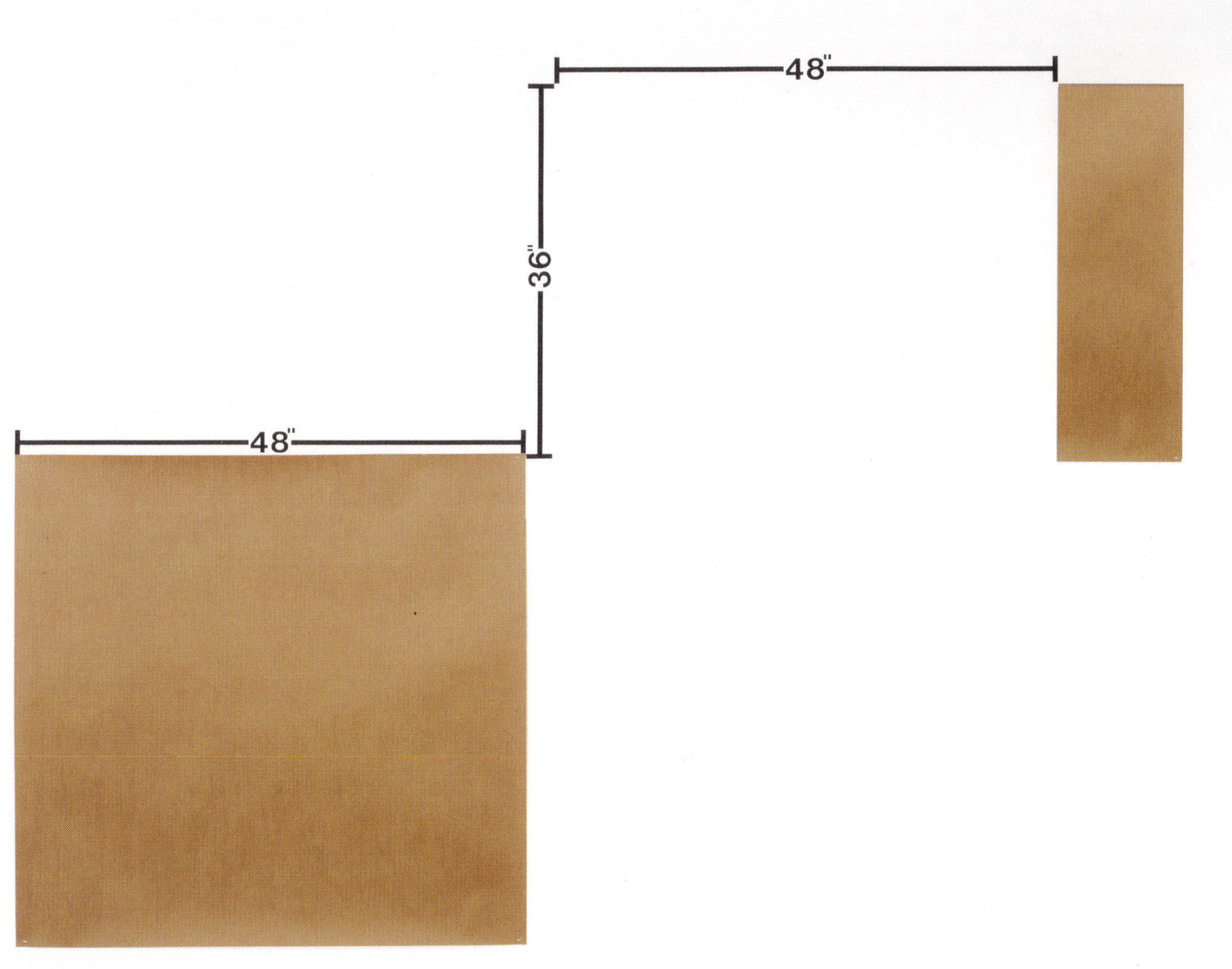
48"
36"
48"

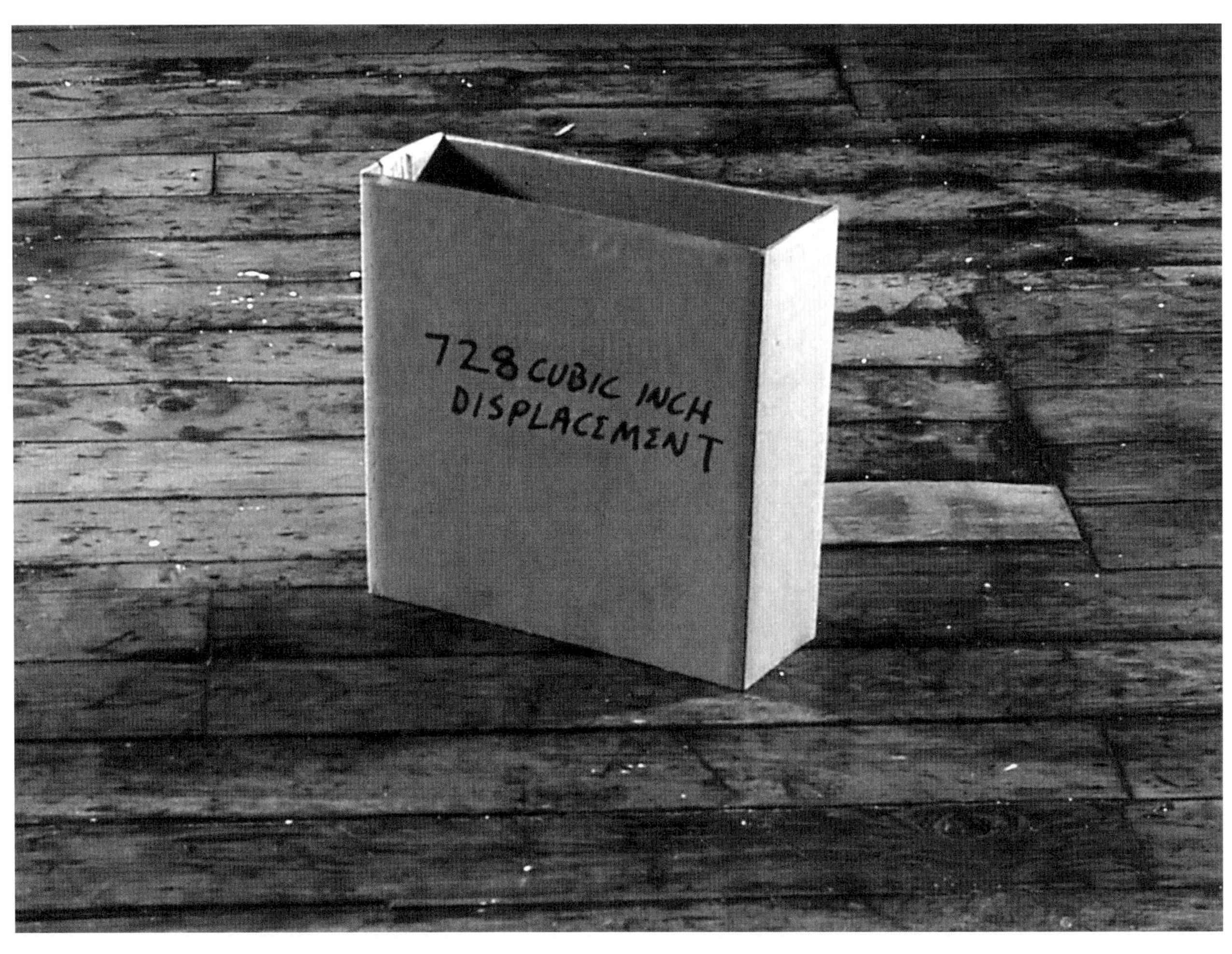

728 Cubic Inch Displacement, 1969

Ink on corrugated cardboard box

16 × 14 × 3¼ inches

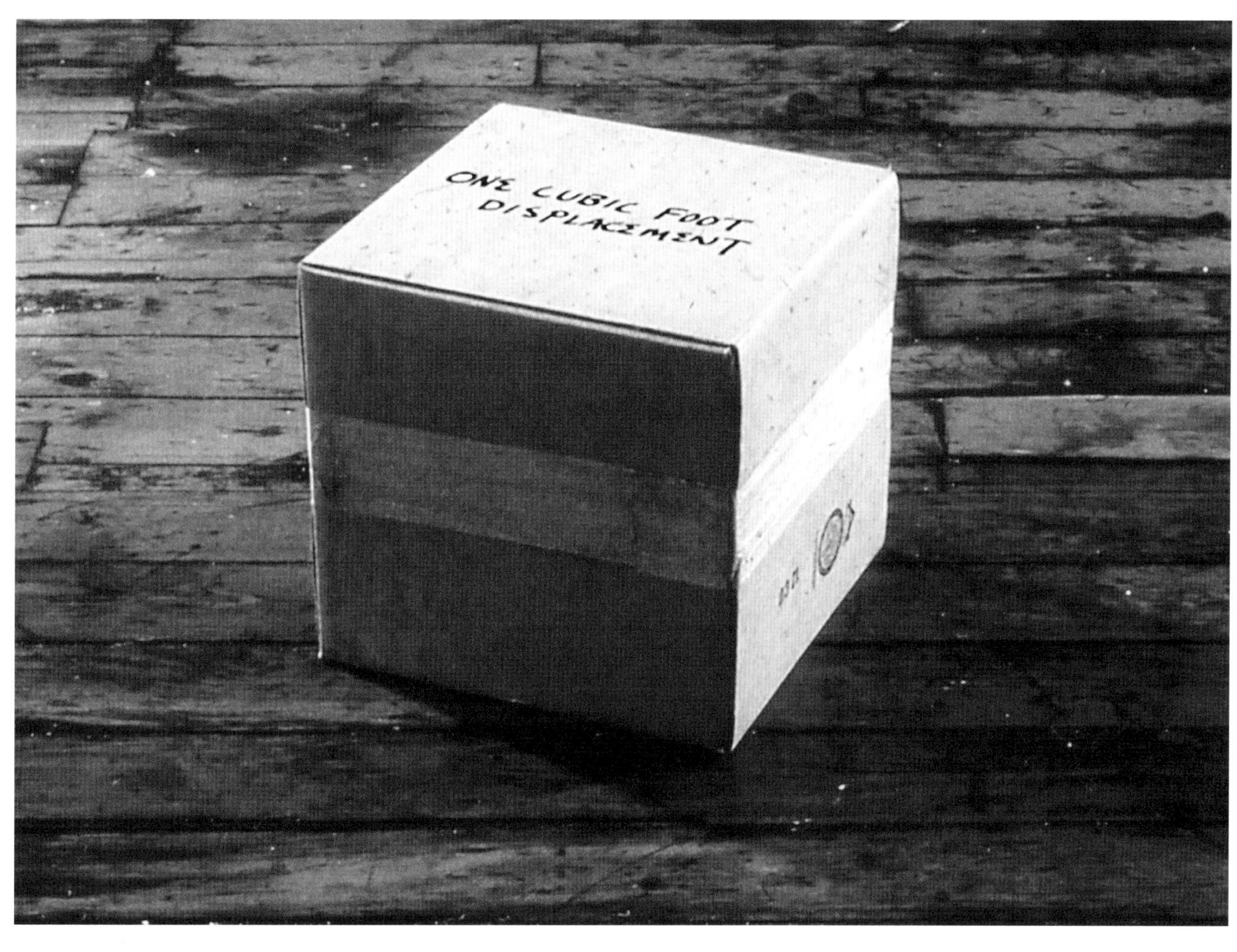

One Cubic Foot Displacement, 1969

Ink on corrugated cardboard box

12 × 12 × 12 inches

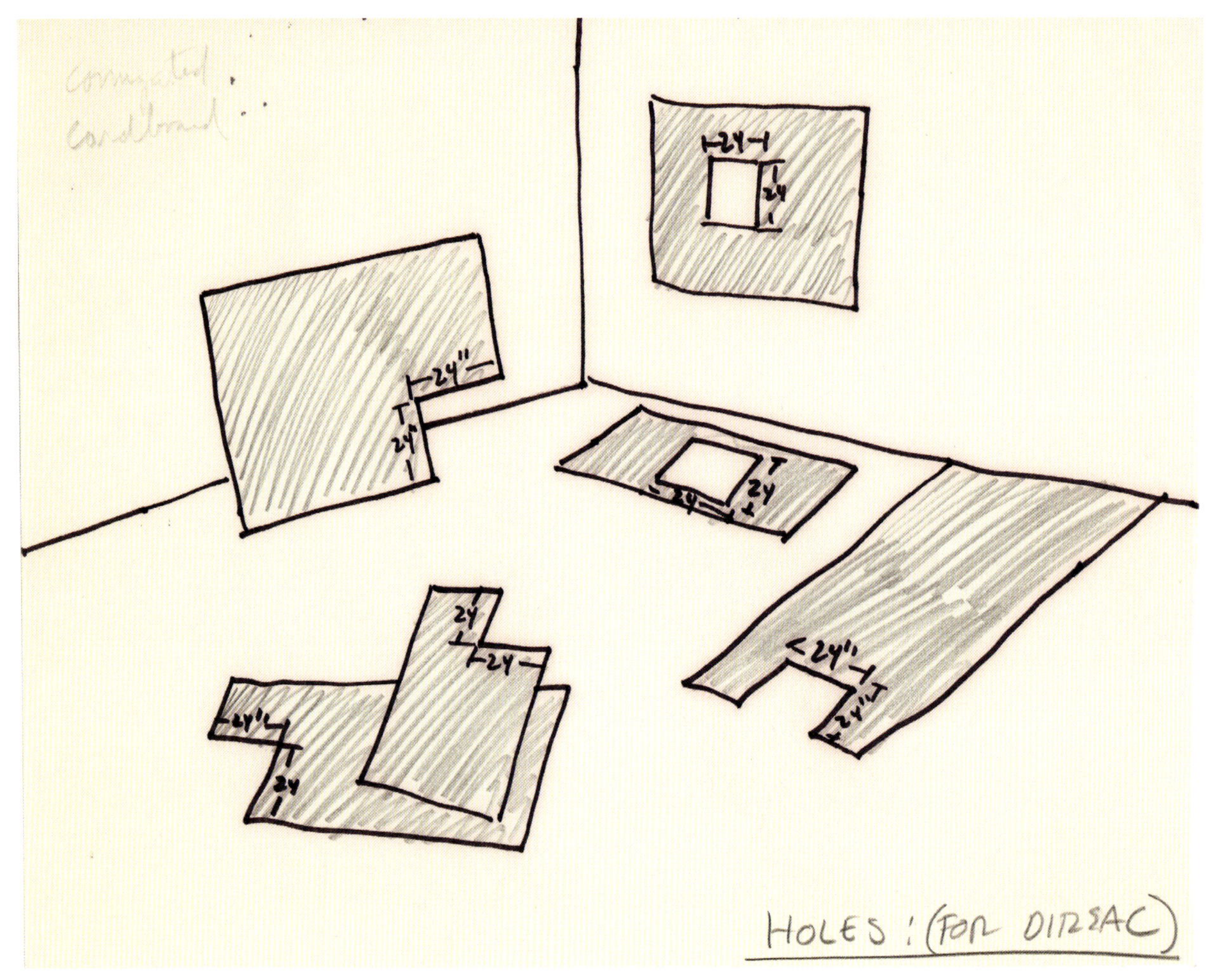

Holes: (For Direac), 1969

Ink and pencil on paper

7¾ × 9½ inches

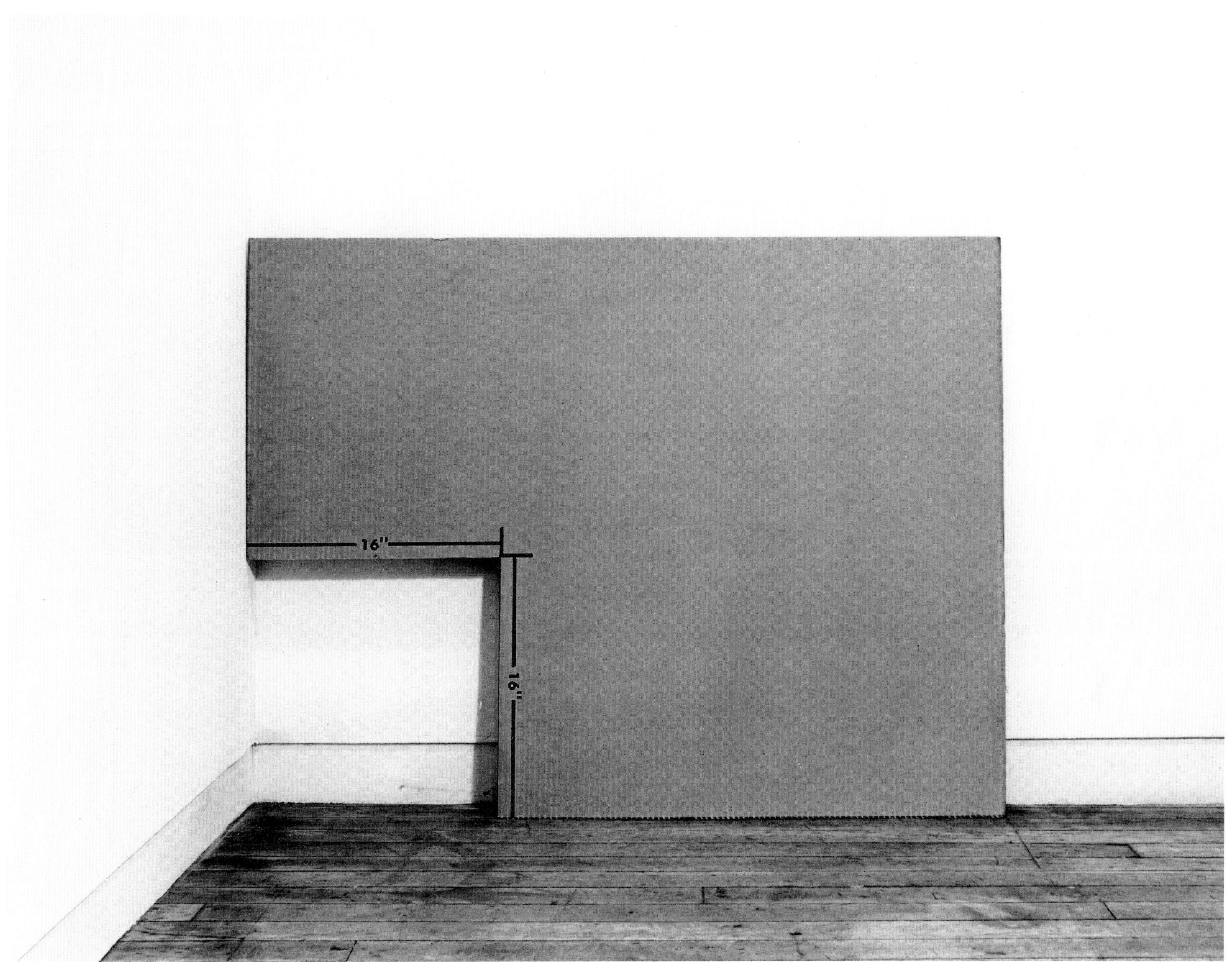

Measurement: Minus 256 Square Inches, 1969

Corrugated cardboard, tape, and Letraset

36 × 48 inches

Installation view, artist's studio, New York

Measurement: 36 Inches + 36 Inches, 1969

Letraset and tape on corrugated cardboard, seven sheets

48 × 72 inches overall

Installation view, artist's studio, New York

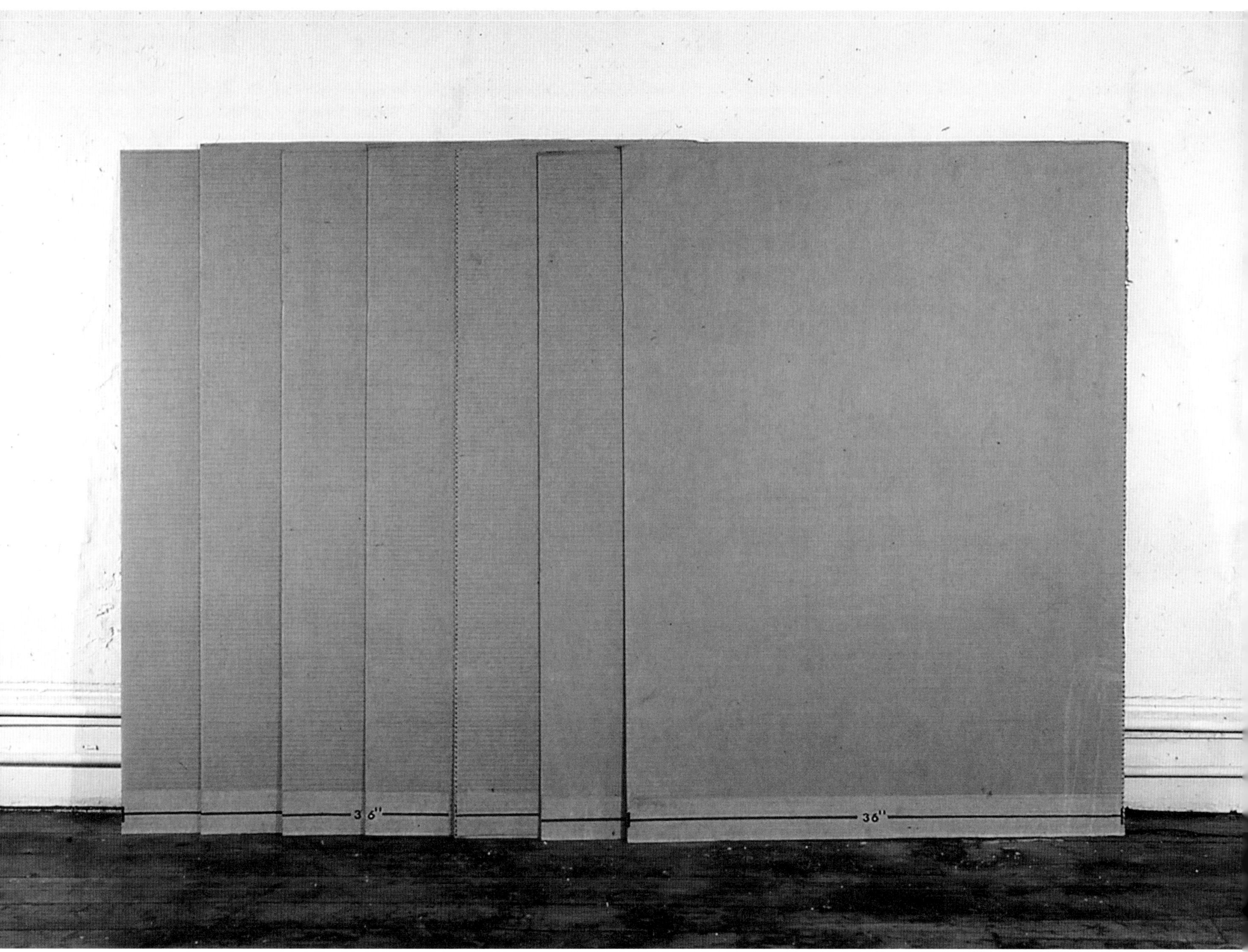
3 6''
36''

Measurement: Two Sheets 36 Inches × 48 Inches, 1969

Letraset on brown paper, taped to corrugated cardboard

48 × 36 inches

Installation view, artist's studio, New York

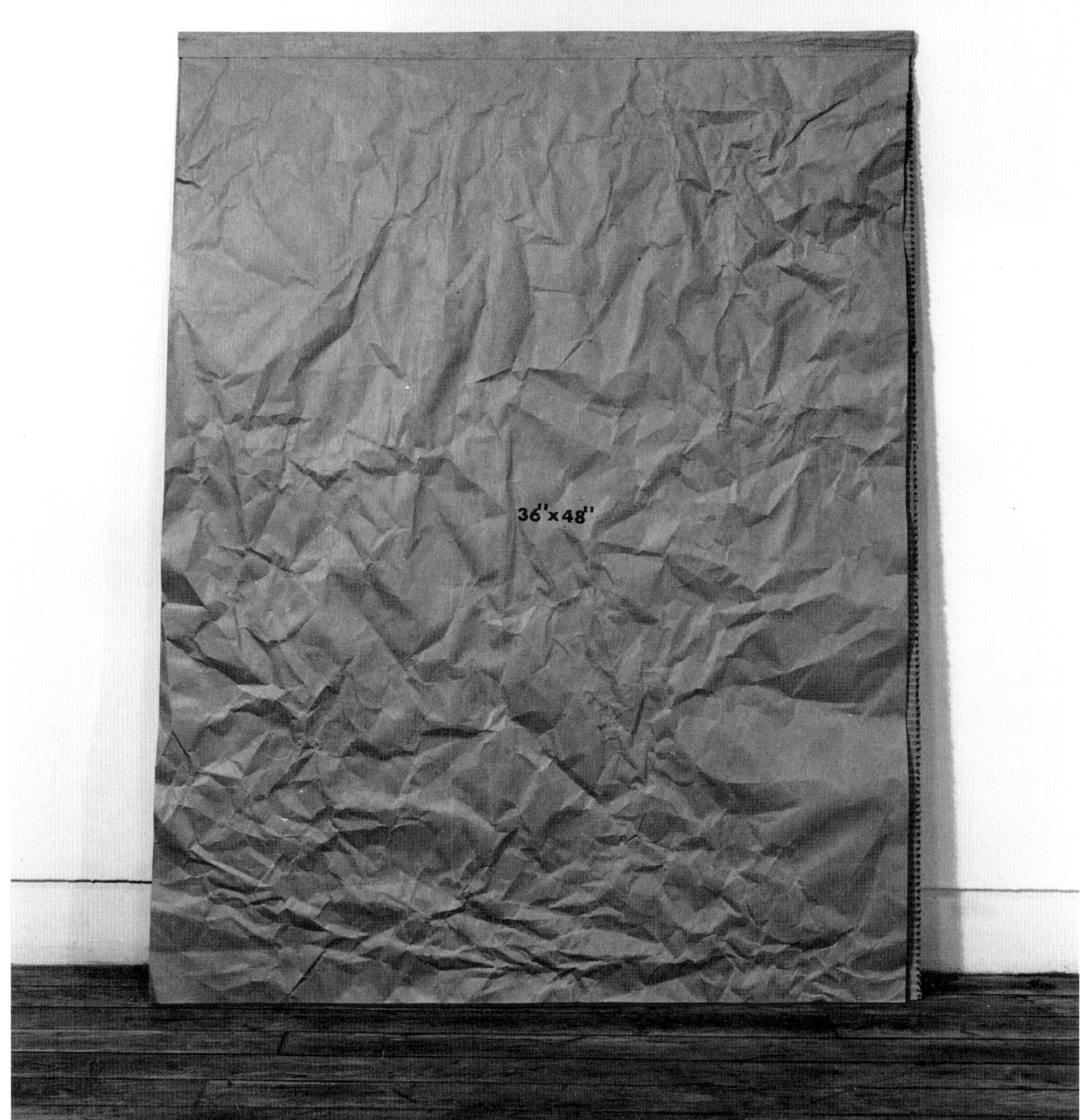
36"x48"

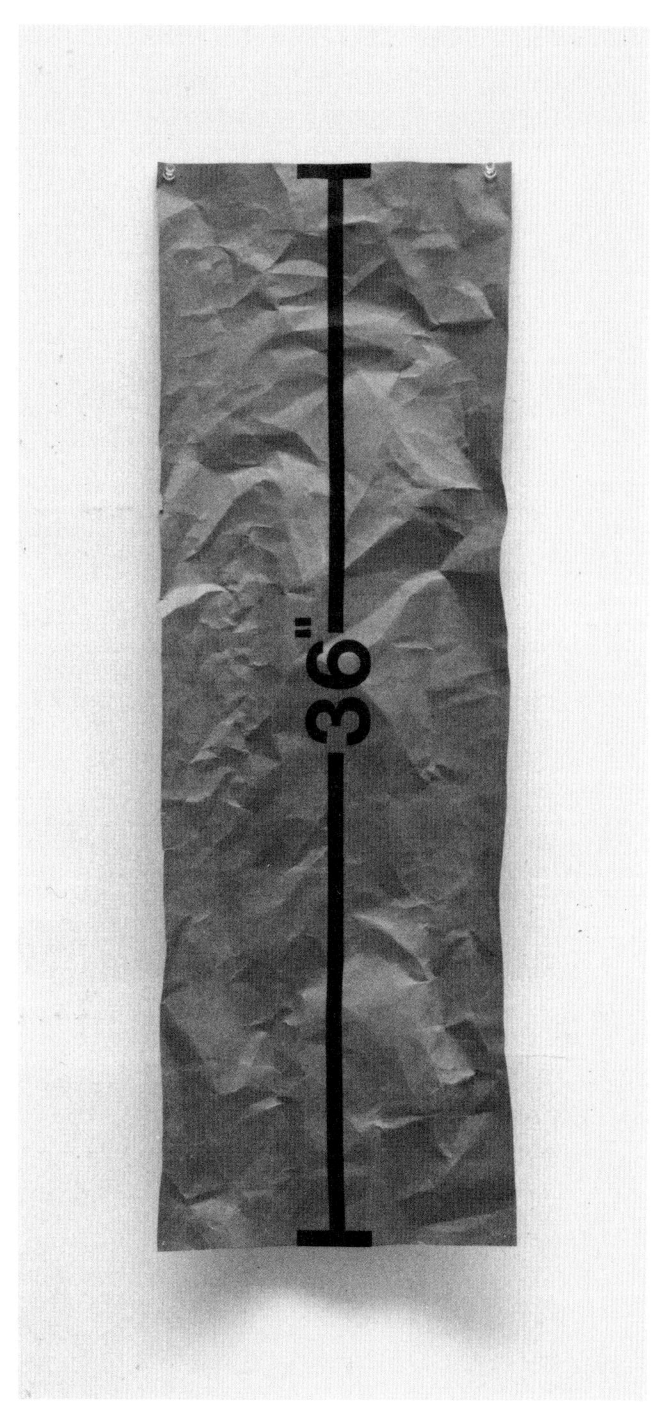

Measurement: Crumpled 36 Inches, 1969

Letraset, tape, and pins on brown paper

36 × 12 inches

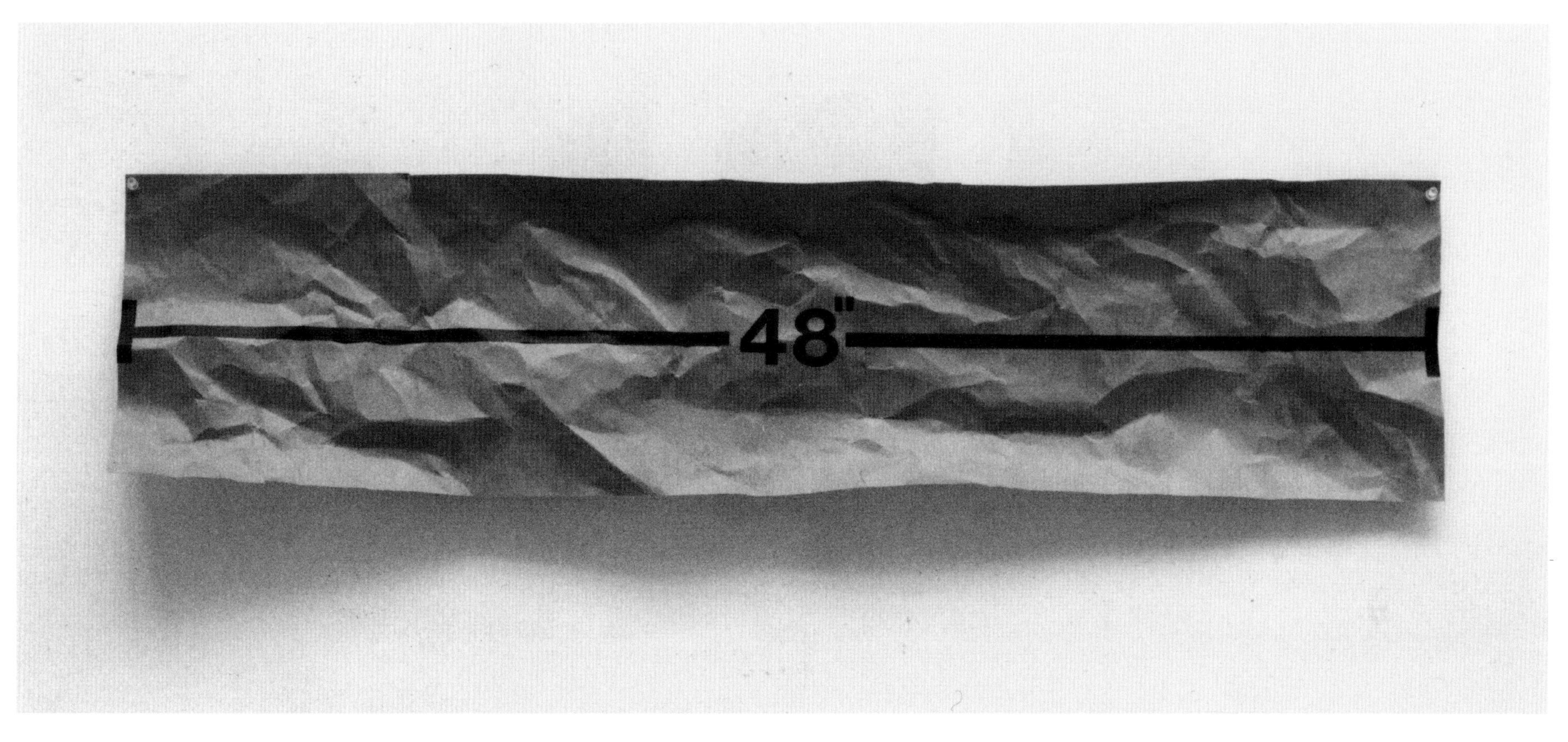

Measurement: Crumpled 48 Inches, 1969

Letraset, tape, and pins on brown paper

12 × 48 inches

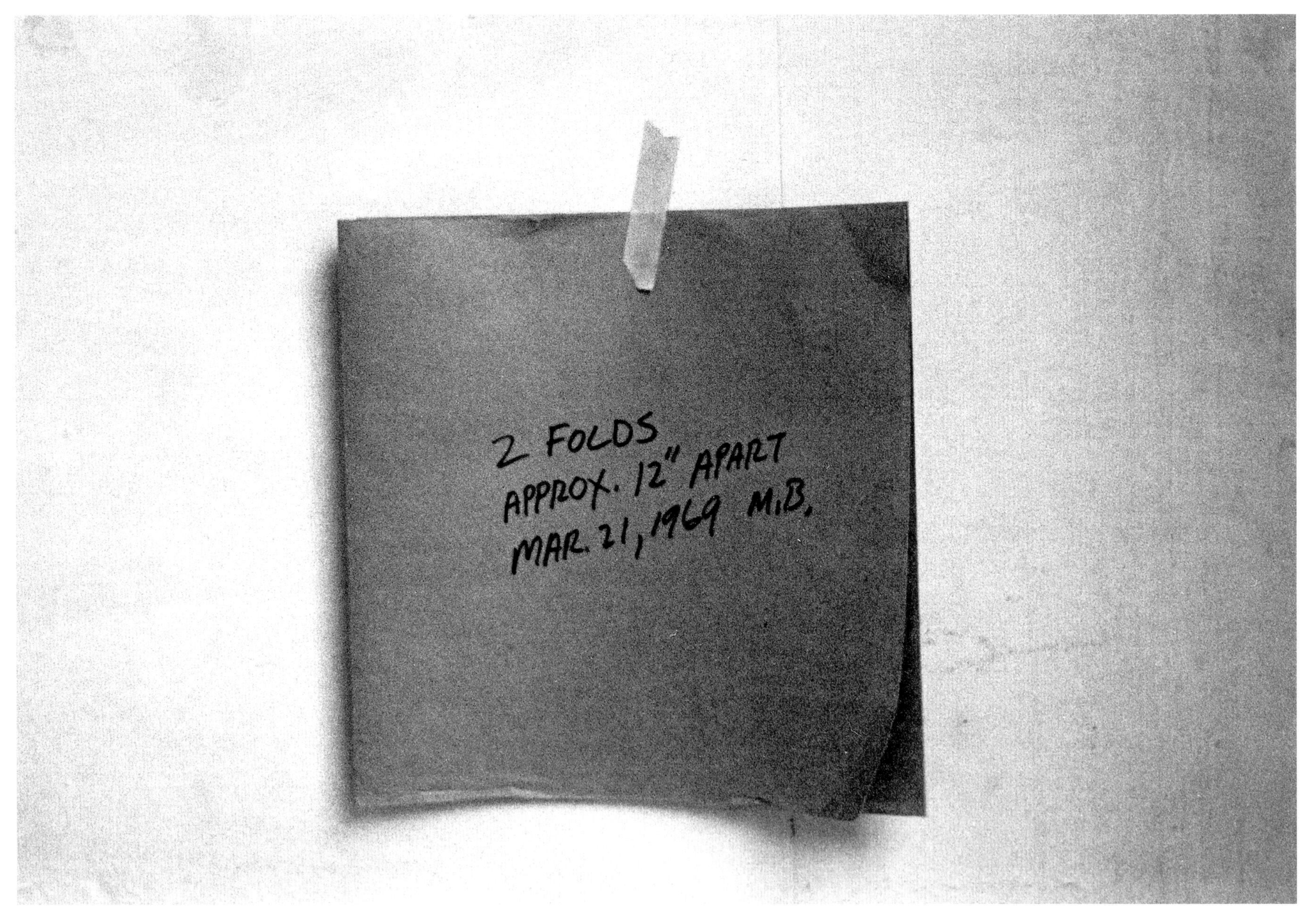

Measurement: Two Folds, 1969
Ink on paper, taped to wall
12 × 12 inches

Measurement: 100 Inches Divided by 4, 1969
Masking tape and crayon on brown paper
100 × 36 inches
Installation view, artist's studio, New York

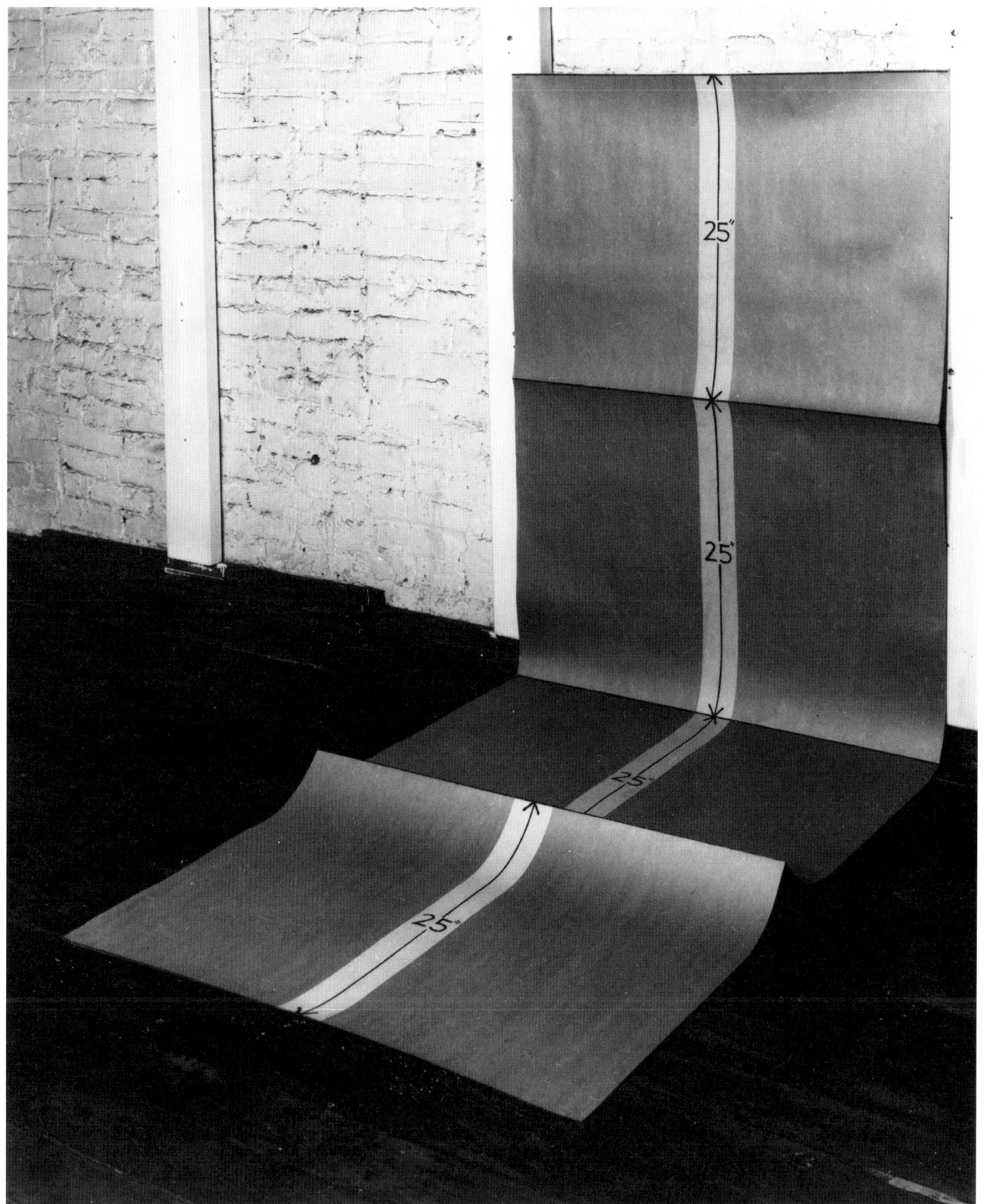
25"
25"
25"
25"

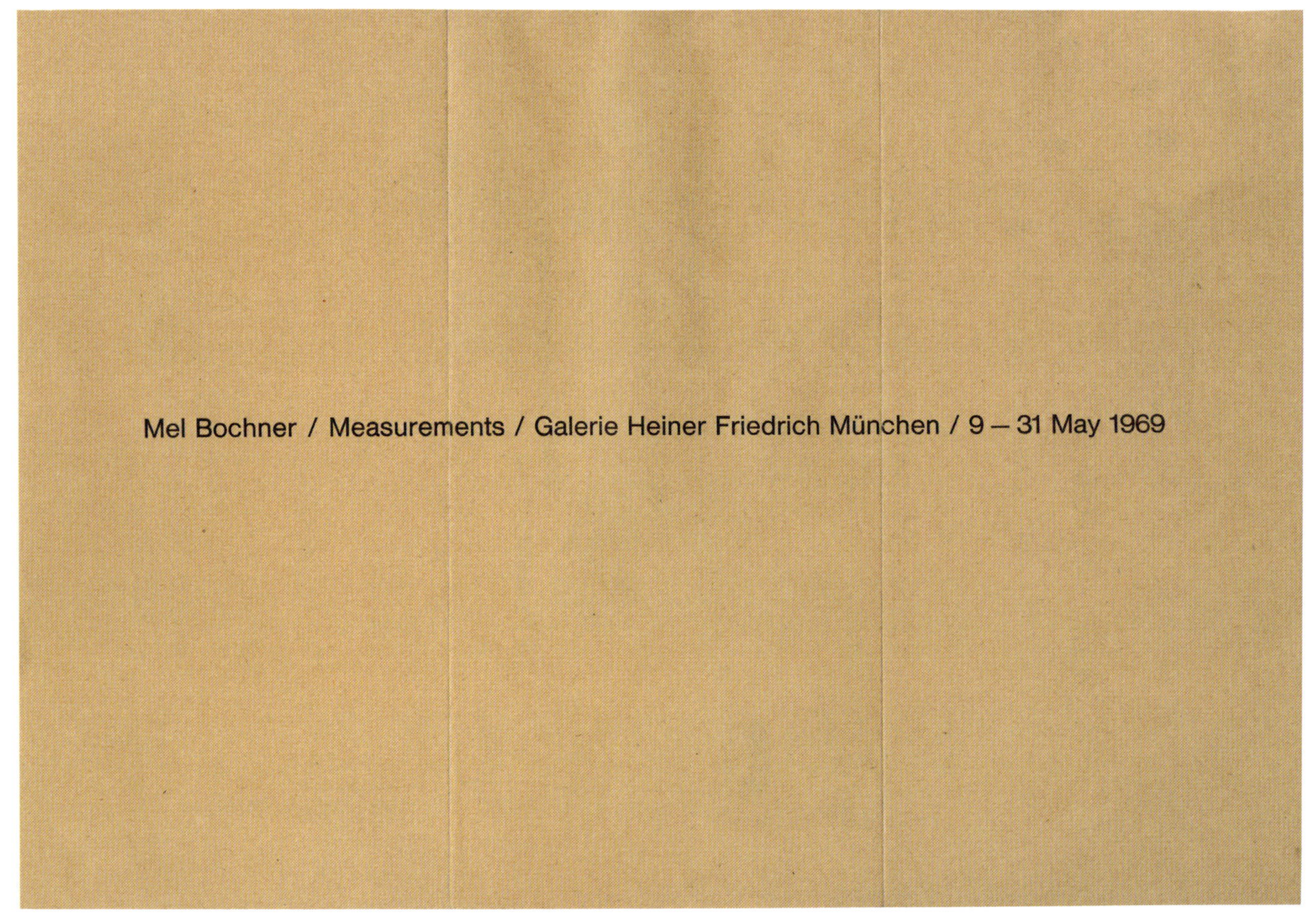

Exhibition Announcement, Galerie Heiner Friedrich, Munich, 1969

Ink on paper (mimeograph), front and back

8¼ × 11¾ inches

MEL BOCHNER

MAXIMILIANSTR. 15
GALERIE HEINER FRIEDRICH
MÜNCHEN

'MEASUREMENTS'

DATES OF EXHIBITION: MAY ~~8~~ 9 - MAY 31 1969

ALL WORKS MADE IN MUNICH DURING THE WEEK OF MAY 1 - MAY 8, 1969

EXHIBITION TO INCLUDE ALL + ONLY THOSE WORKS POSSIBLE TO MAKE IN ~~a~~ ONE ~~w~~ WEEK WITH MATERIAL AVAILABLE

THREE PROCEDURAL GROUPS TO BE WORKED ~~[illegible]~~ FROM

GROUP 'A': EXTERIORATED MEASUREMENTS — ANY OBJECT, MATERIAL OR PLACE (STABLE) ORIENTED TO A SYSTEM OUTSIDE ~~[illegible]~~ ITSELF ~~[illegible]~~ — (DECLARATION OF POSITION) CO-ORDINATED

GROUP 'B': SITUATED MEASUREMENTS ~~the~~ THE MEASUREMENTS OF A STABLE OBJECT OR PLACE MARK DIRECTLY ONTO IT, (SUPER-IMPOSED)

GROUP 'C': COMPARATIVE MEASUREMENTS ANY STABLE OBJECT, MATERIAL OR PLACE RELATED TO PRE-DETERMINED GIVEN STANDARD ~~(ROOM DIM)~~ (SECTIONED)

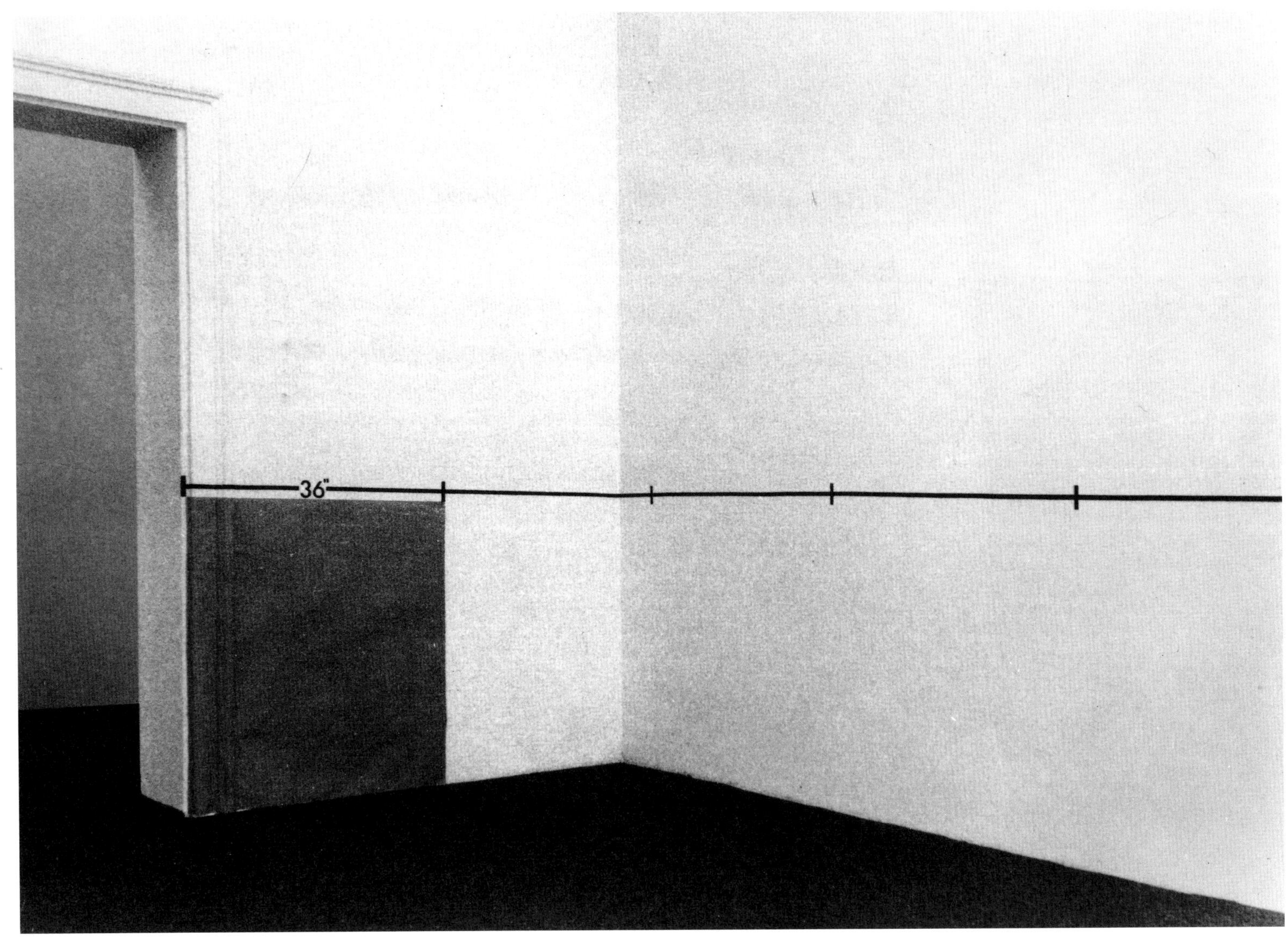

This spread and following pages

36 Inch Latitudinal Projection, 1969

Letraset, tape, and brown paper stapled to wall

Dimensions variable

Tate Modern, London, Presented by the Tate Americas Foundation 2016

Installation views, *Measurements*, Galerie Heiner Friedrich, Munich, 1969

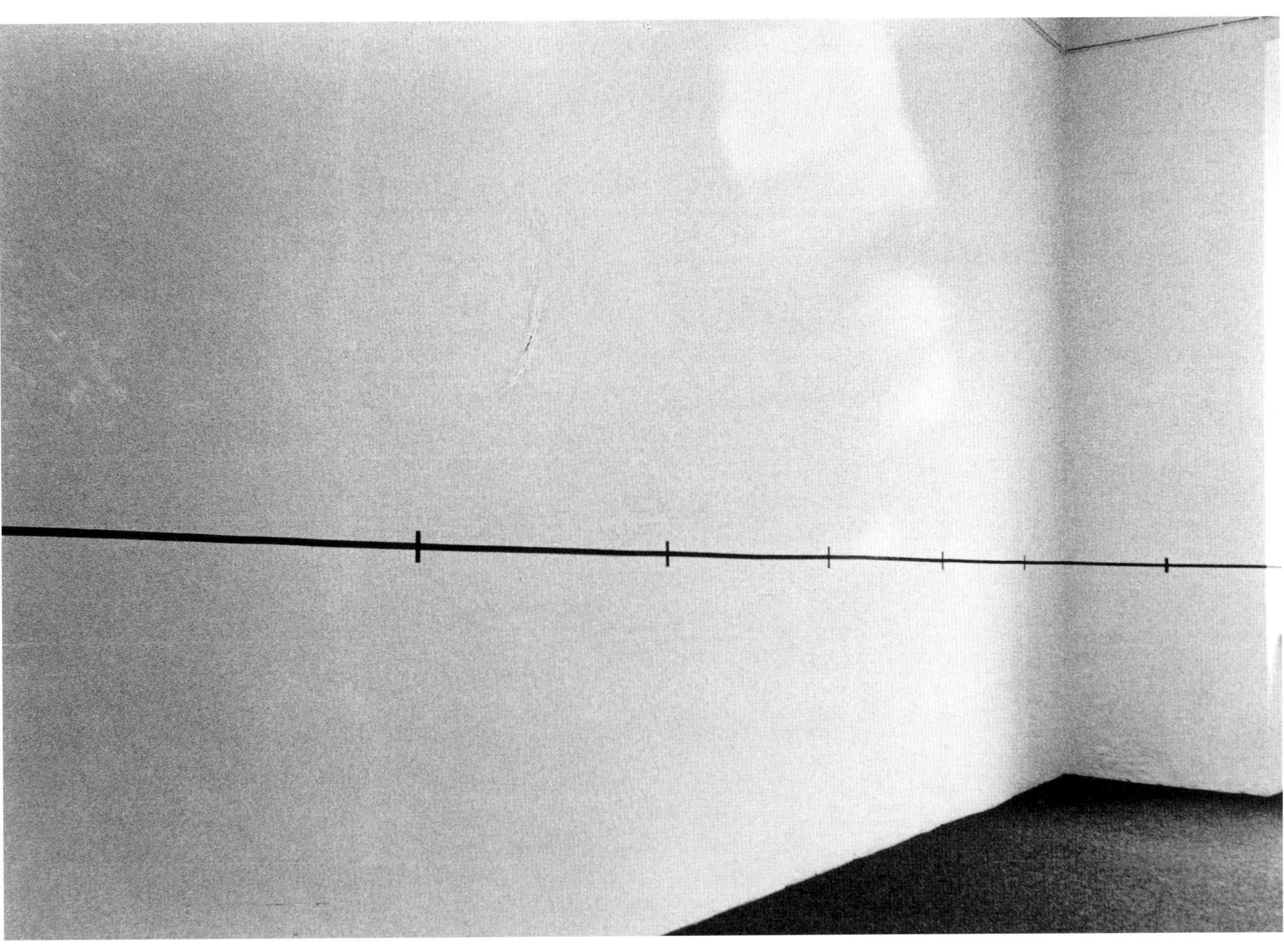

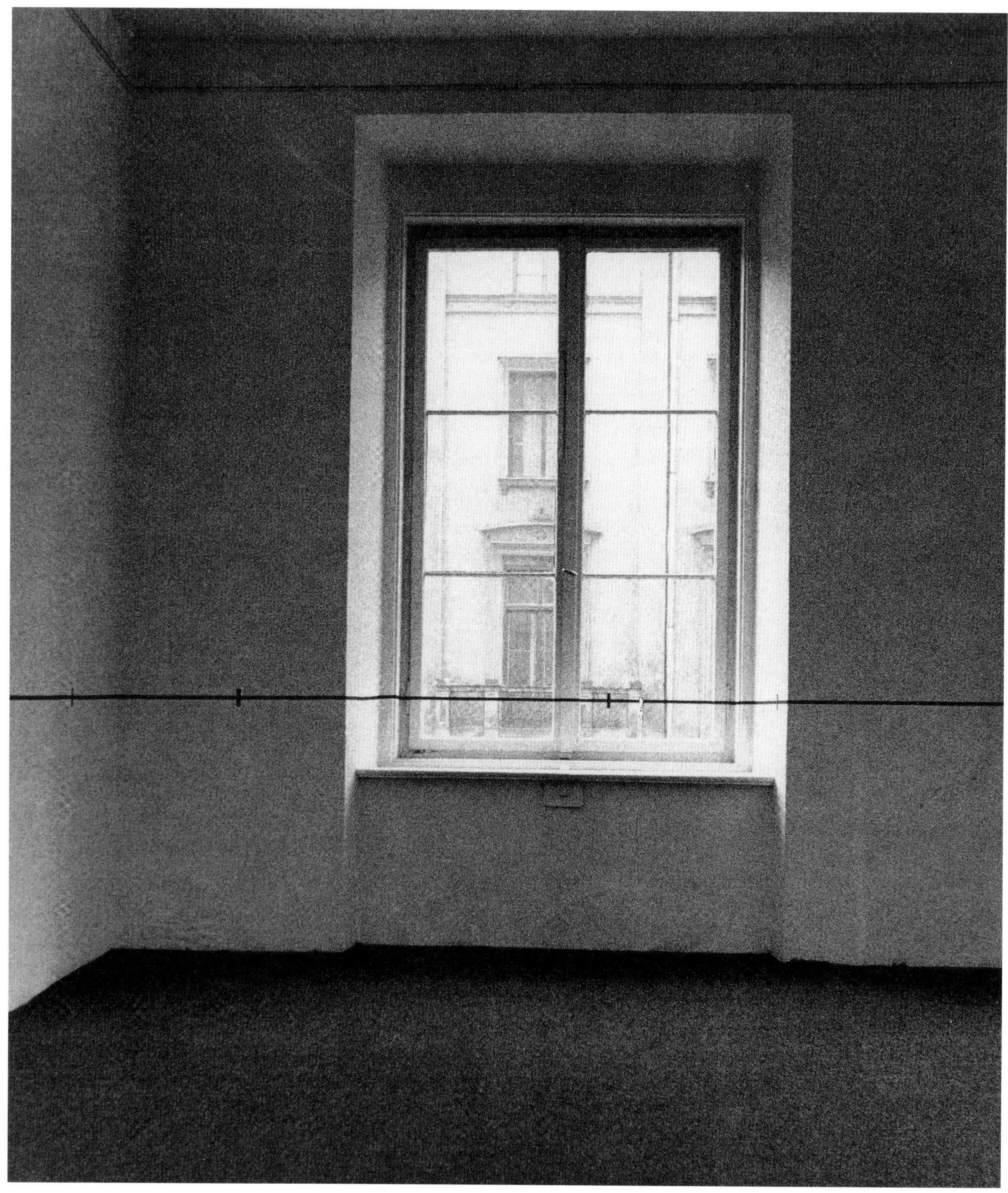

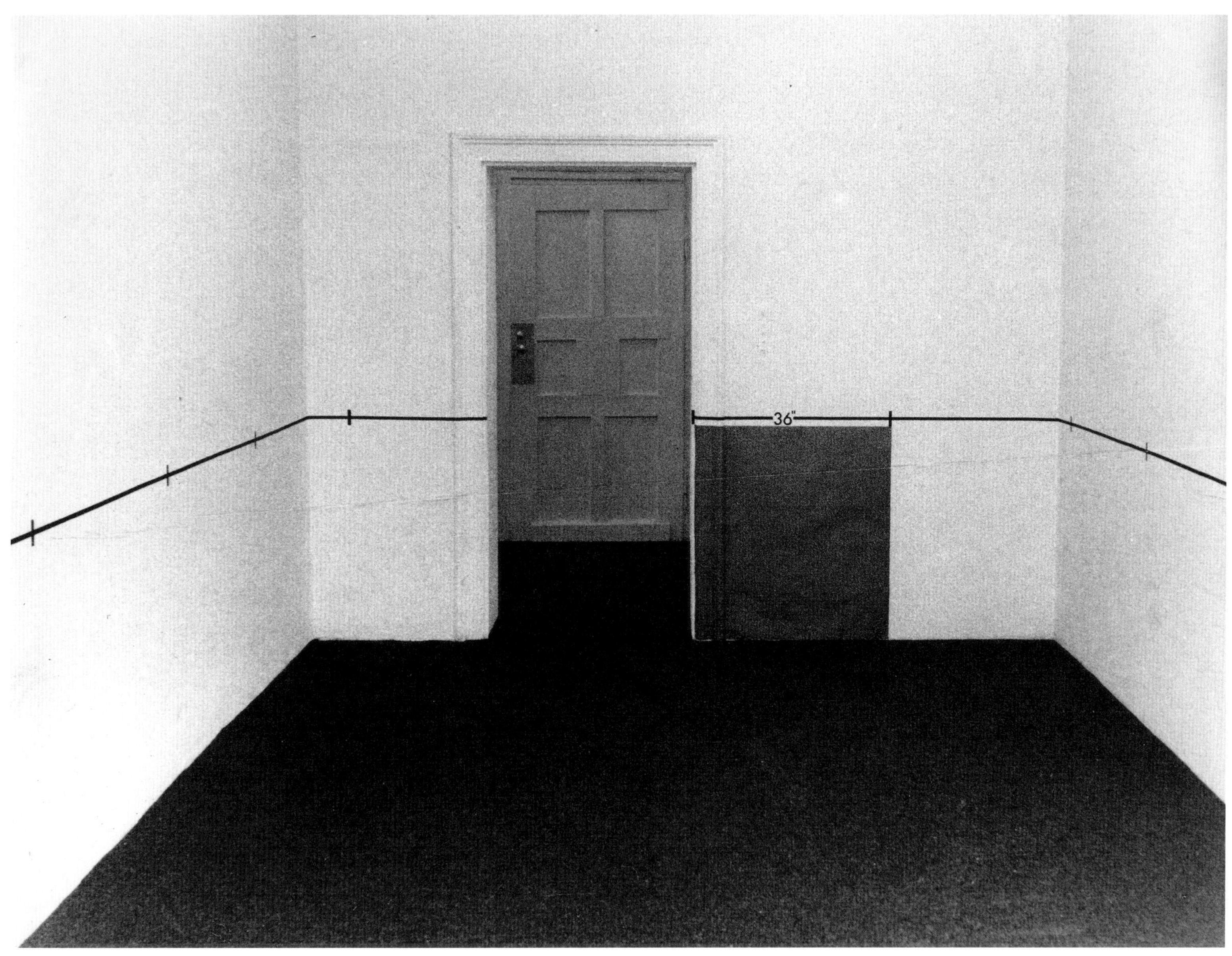
36"

This spread and following pages

Measurement: Room, 1969

Letraset and tape on wall

Dimensions variable

Museum of Modern Art, New York, Committee on Painting and Sculpture Funds

Installation views, *Measurements*, Galerie Heiner Friedrich, Munich, 1969

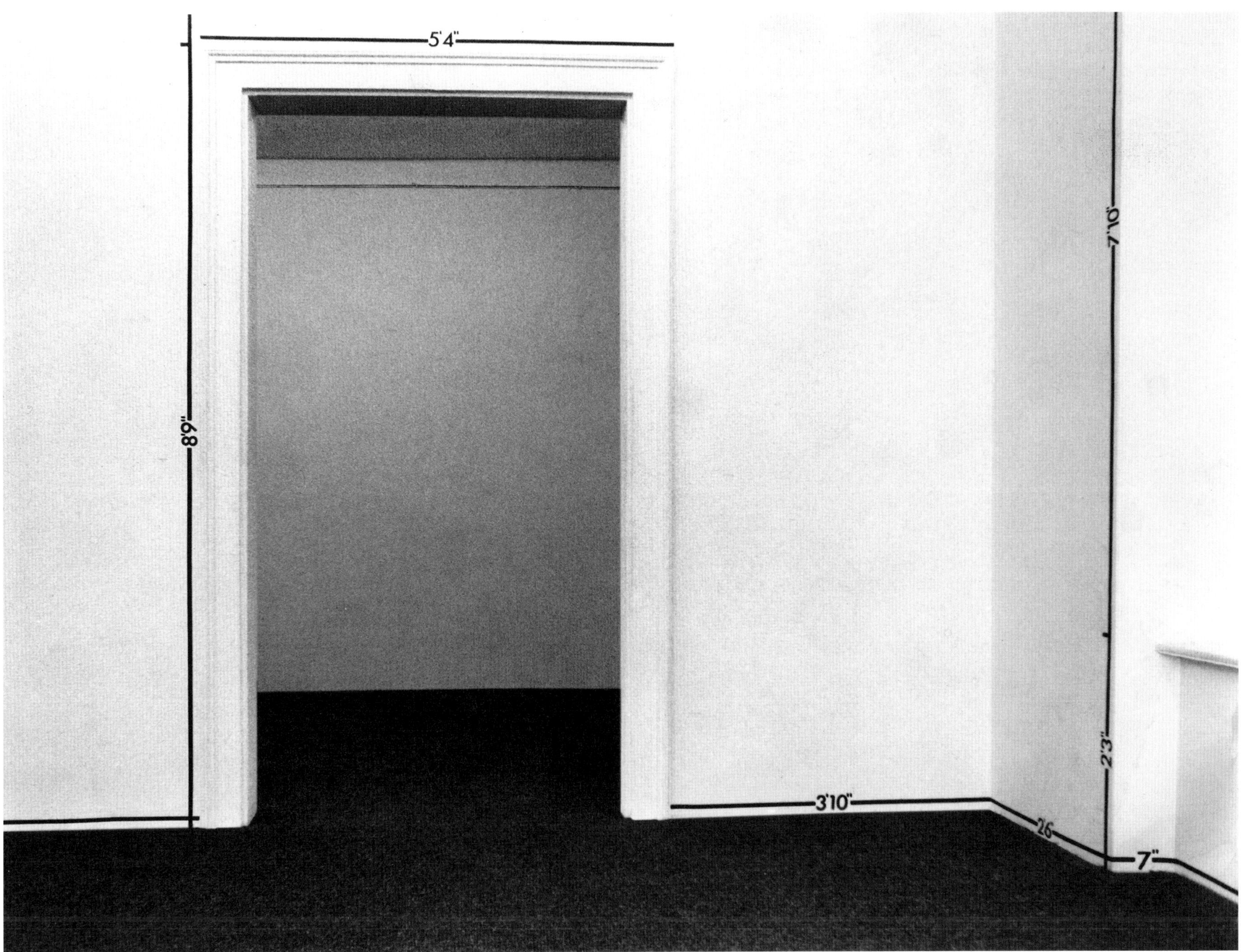
5'4"
8'9"
7'10"
2'3"
3'10"
26
7"

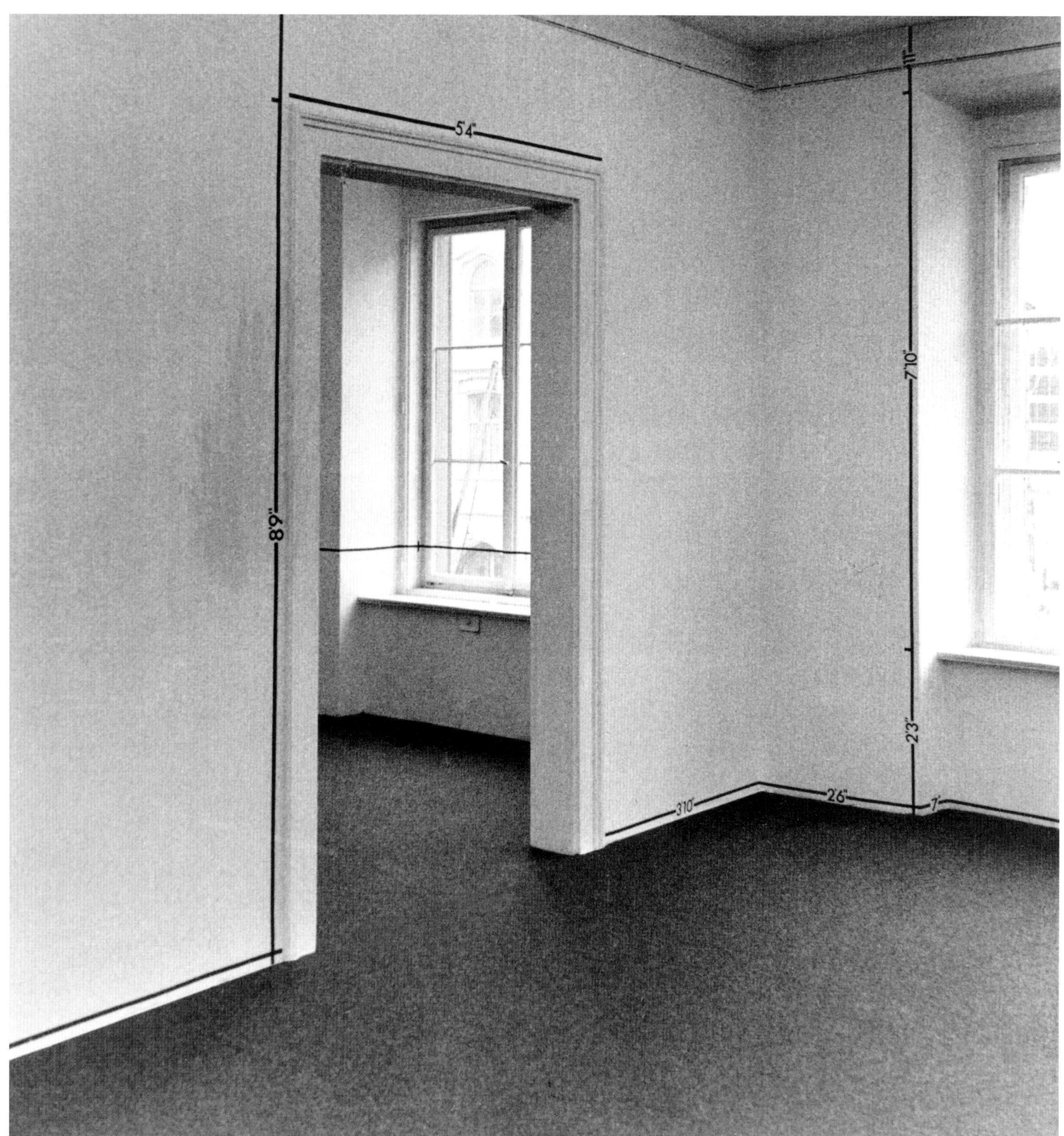
5'4"
8'9"
7'10"
2'3"
3'10"
2'6"
7"

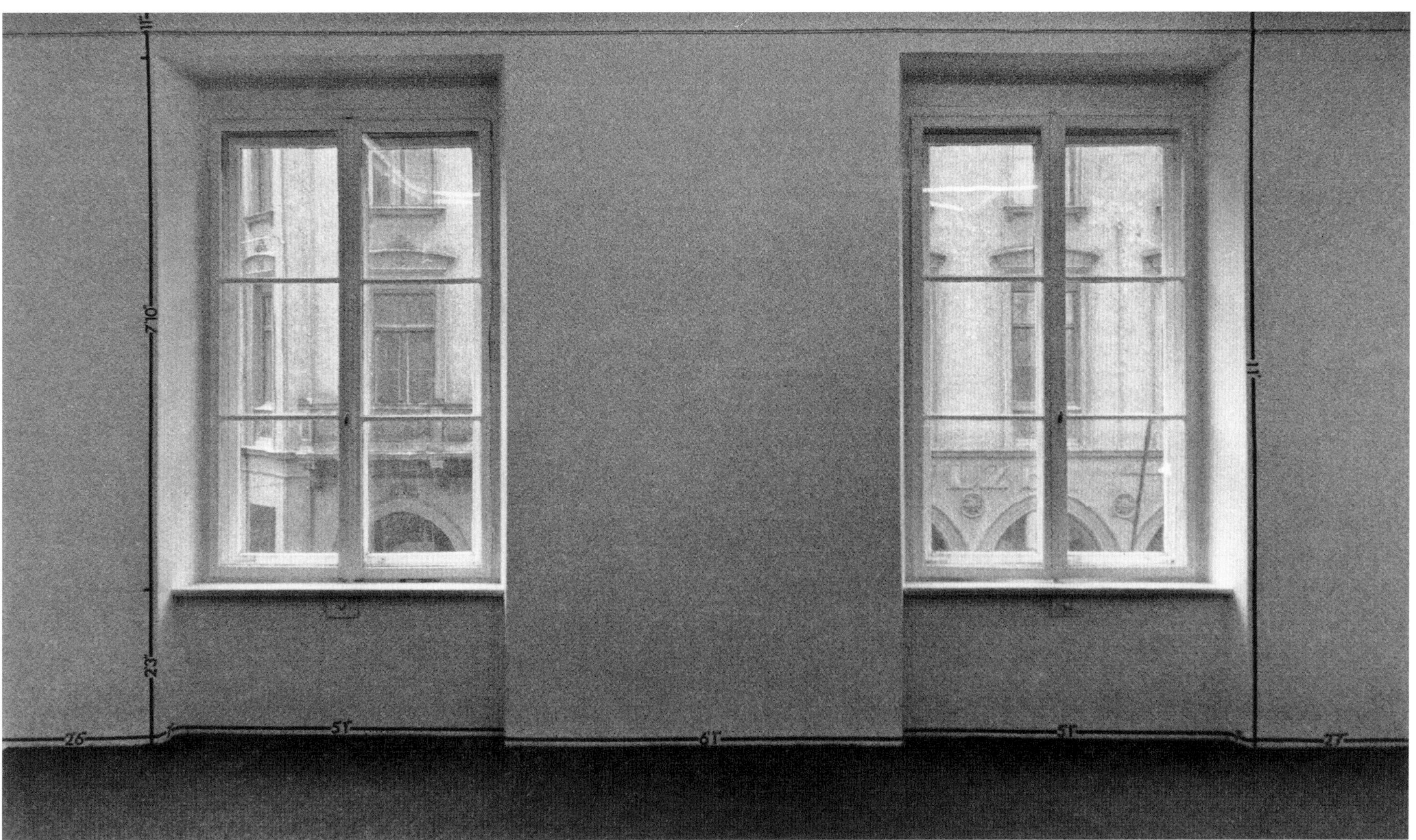

11'
7'10"
2'3"
26
5'1"
6'1"
5'1"
2'7"
11'

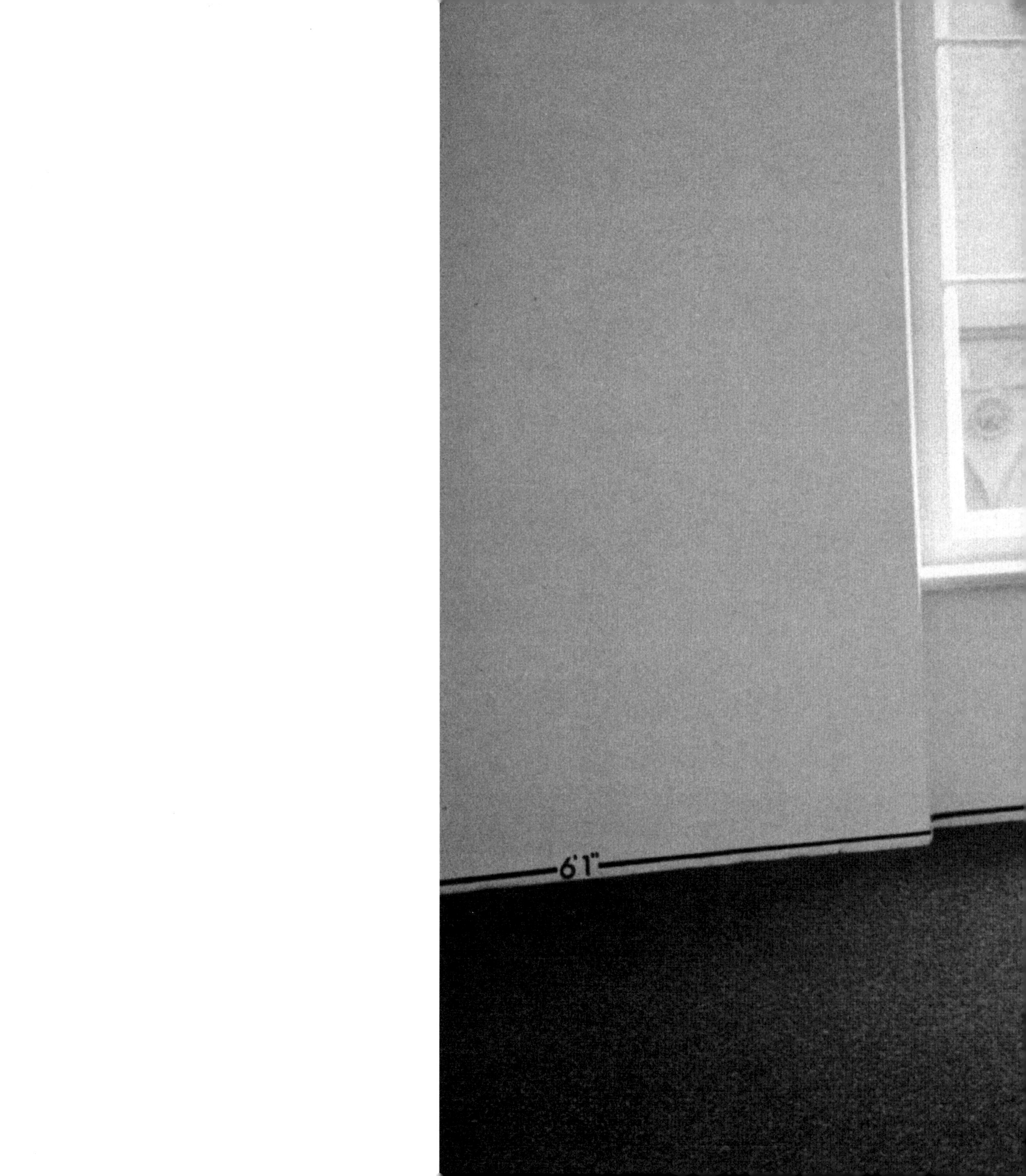
6'1"

11'
5'1"
7
2'7"
3'10"

2'3"
5'4"
8'9"
3'10"

10'10"

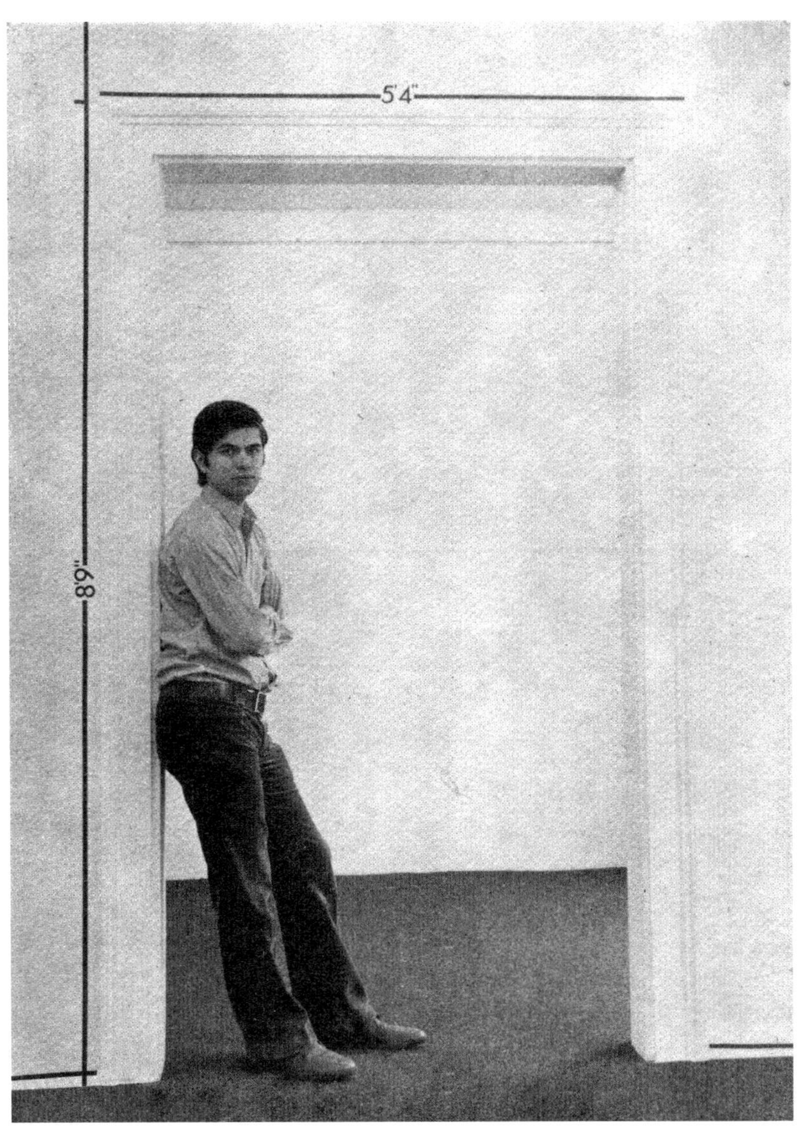

Exhibition announcement, Konrad Fischer Galerie, Düsseldorf, West Germany, 1969

Offset lithograph

4¼ × 5⅞ inches

MEL BOCHNER

MEASURED ROOM SERIES:

48 " LONGITUDINAL PROJECTION

BEI

KONRAD FISCHER

DÜSSELDORF

NEUBRÜCKSTR. 12

TEL. 32 14 64

VOM 22. MAI BIS 6. JUNI

ERÖFFNUNG: DONNERSTAG, 22. 5., 20 UHR

MEL BOCHNER AUS NEW YORK IST DA

DRUCKSACHE

Study for Konrad Fischer Galerie Installation, 1969

Ink on graph paper

4 × 6½ inches

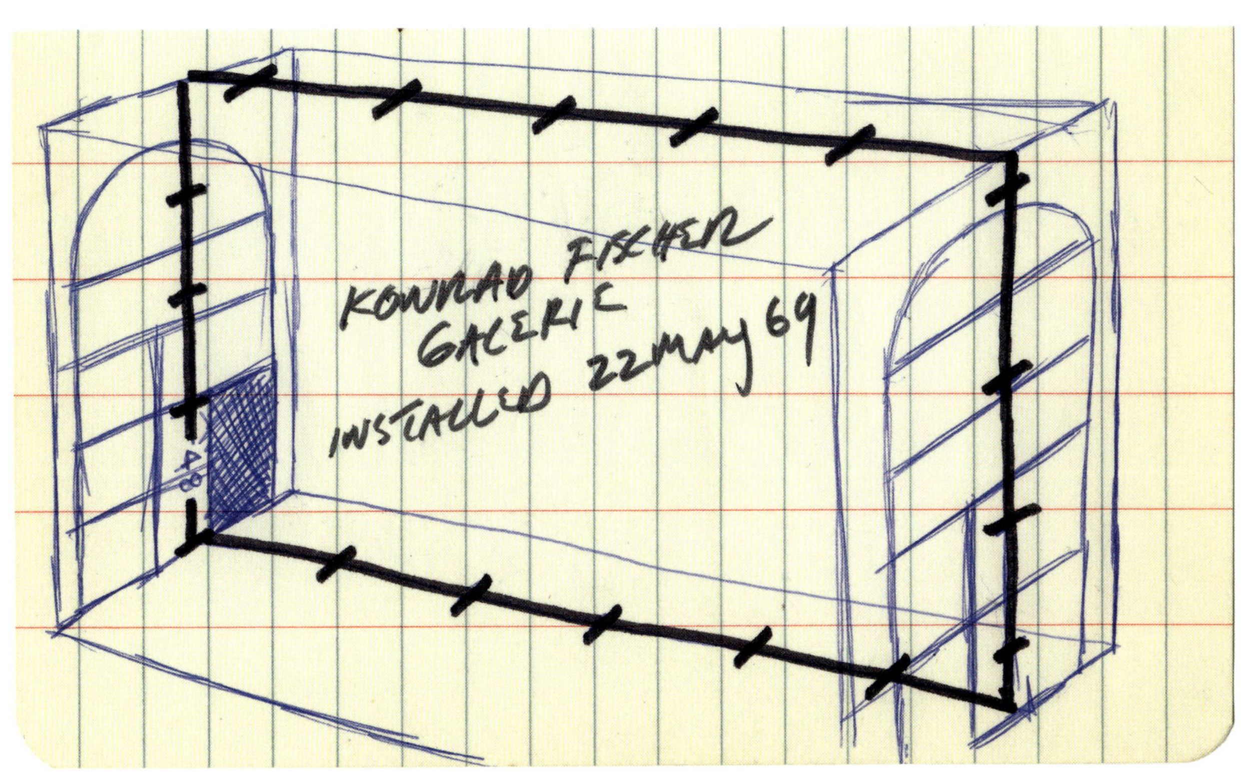
KONRAD FISCHER
GALERIE
INSTALLED 22 MAY 69

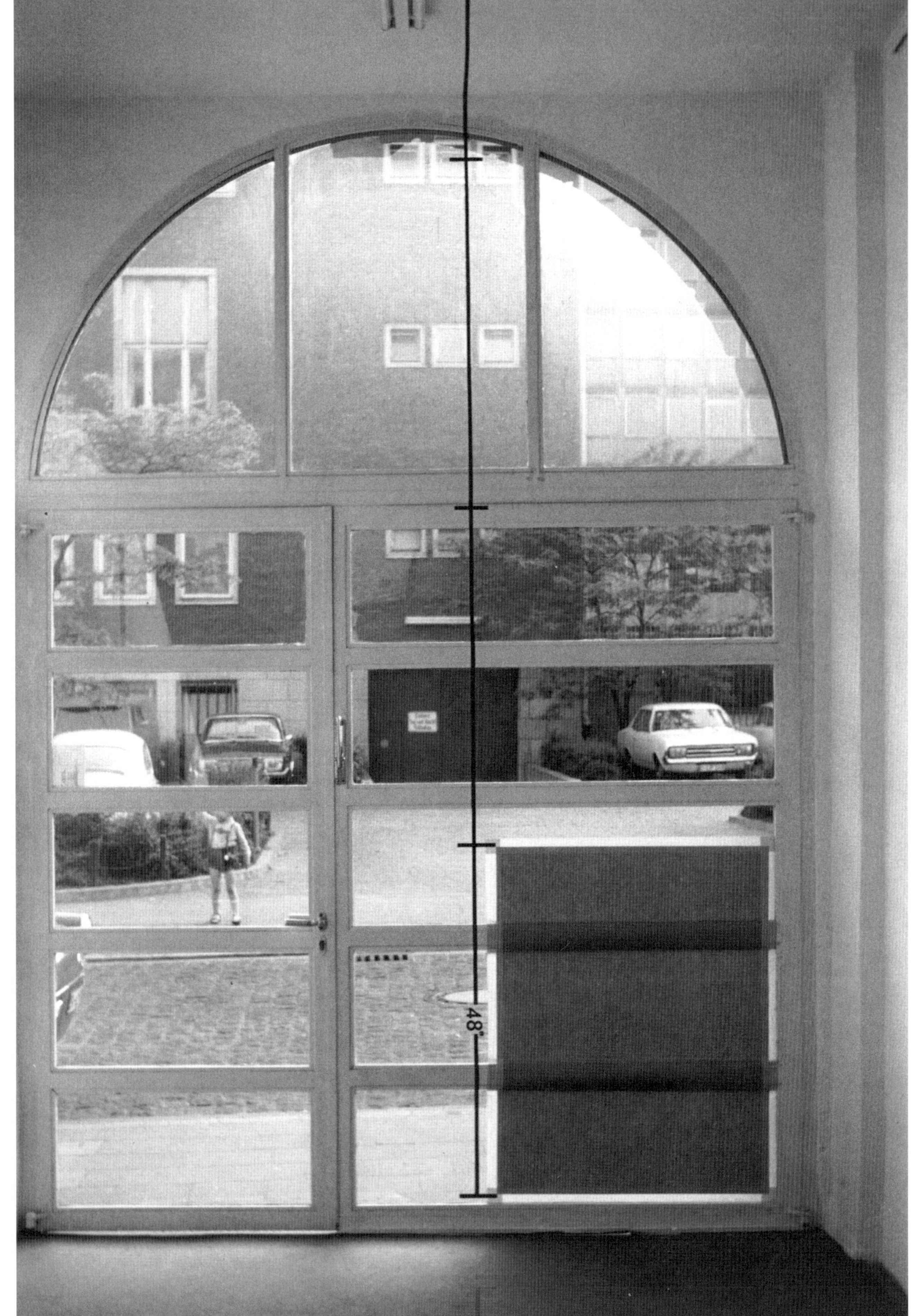
48"

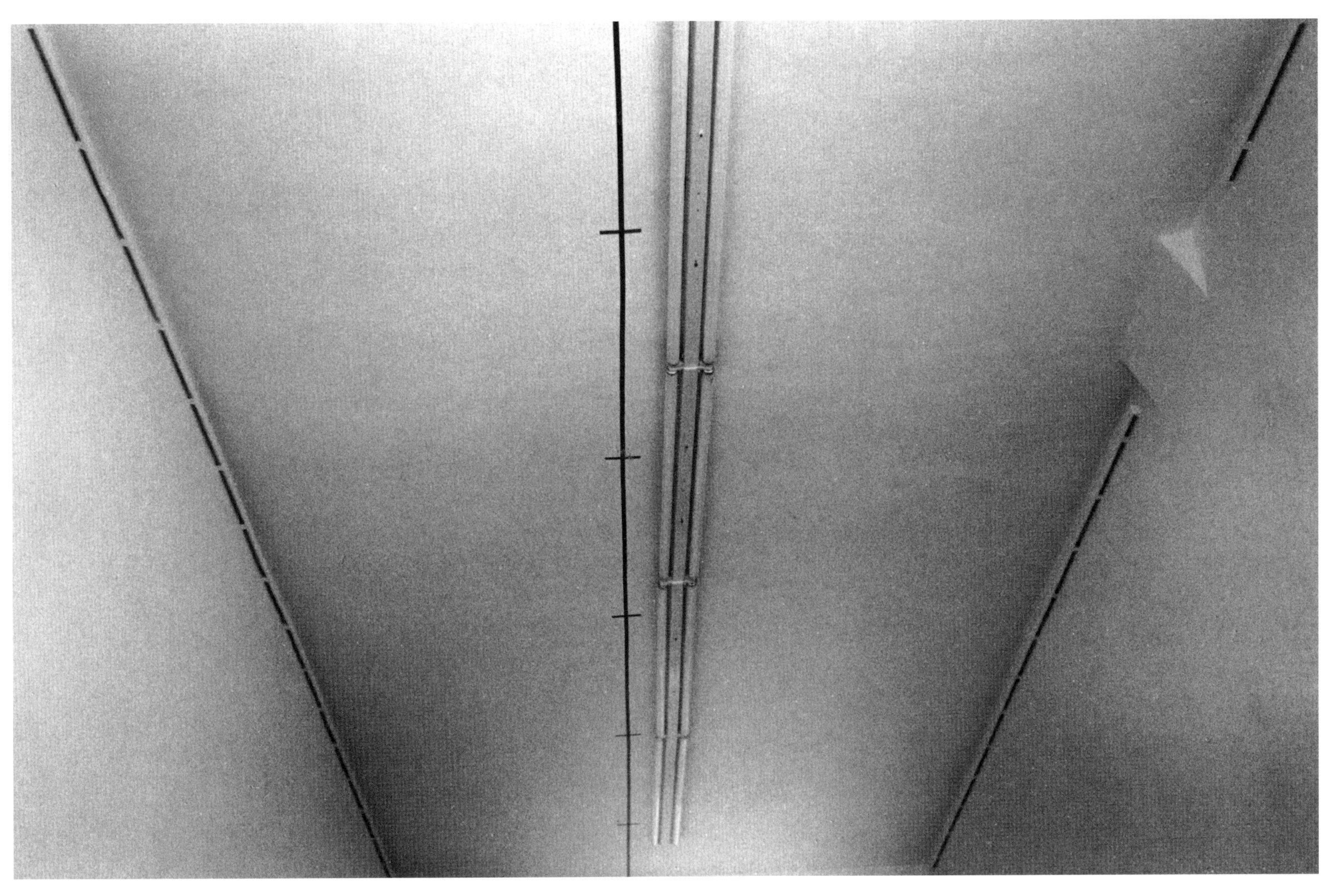

48 Inch Longitudinal Projection, 1969
Brown paper, Letraset, and tape on wall, ceiling, floor, and window
Installation views, *Mel Bochner: Measured Room Series: 48" Longitudinal Projection*, Konrad Fischer Galerie, Düsseldorf, West Germany, 1969

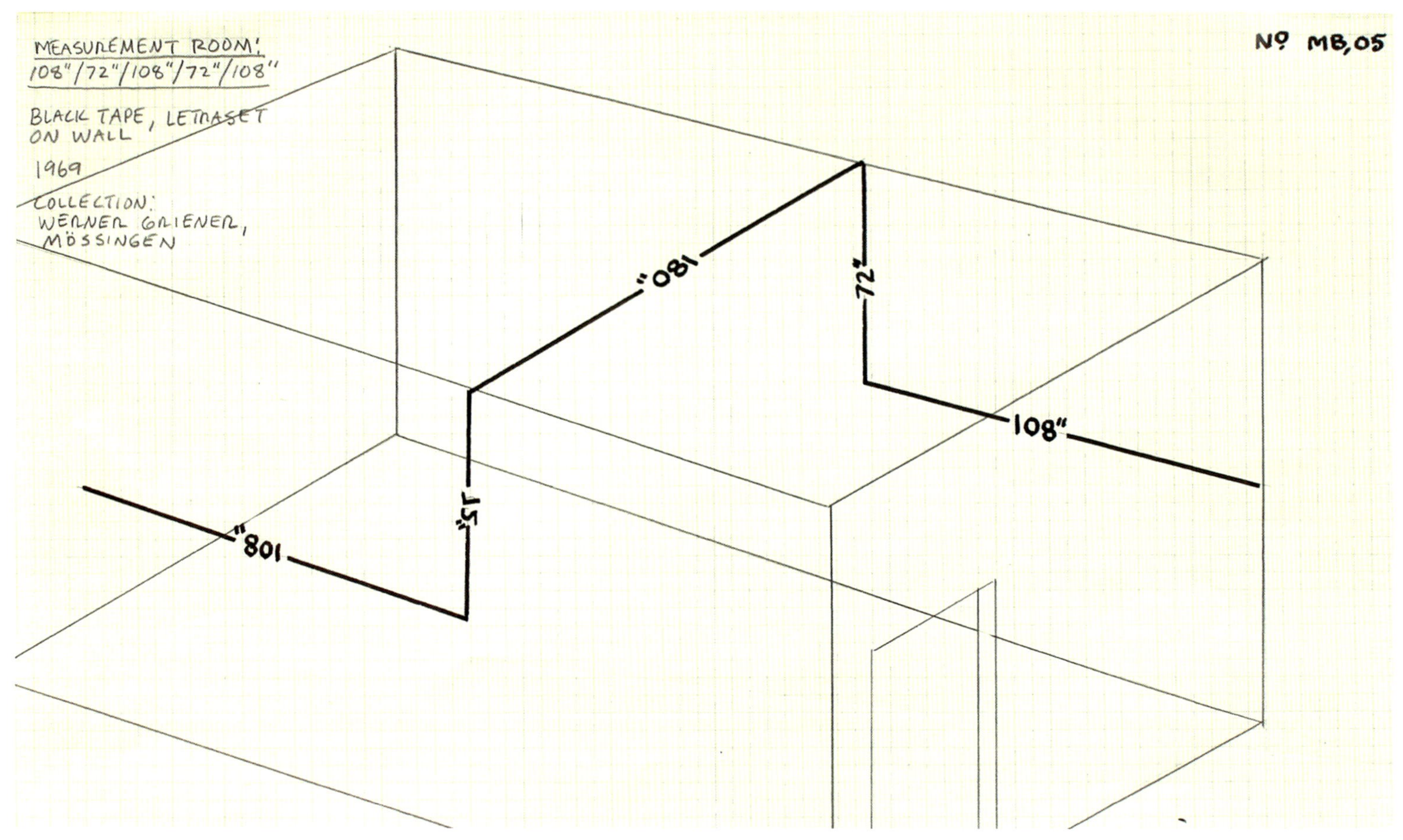

Study for Measurement: Room, 1969
Pencil and ink on graph paper
7½ × 12¼ inches

108 × 72 × 180 × 72 × 108 Inches, 1969
Letraset and tape on wall
Collection of Werner Greiner, Mössingen, Germany

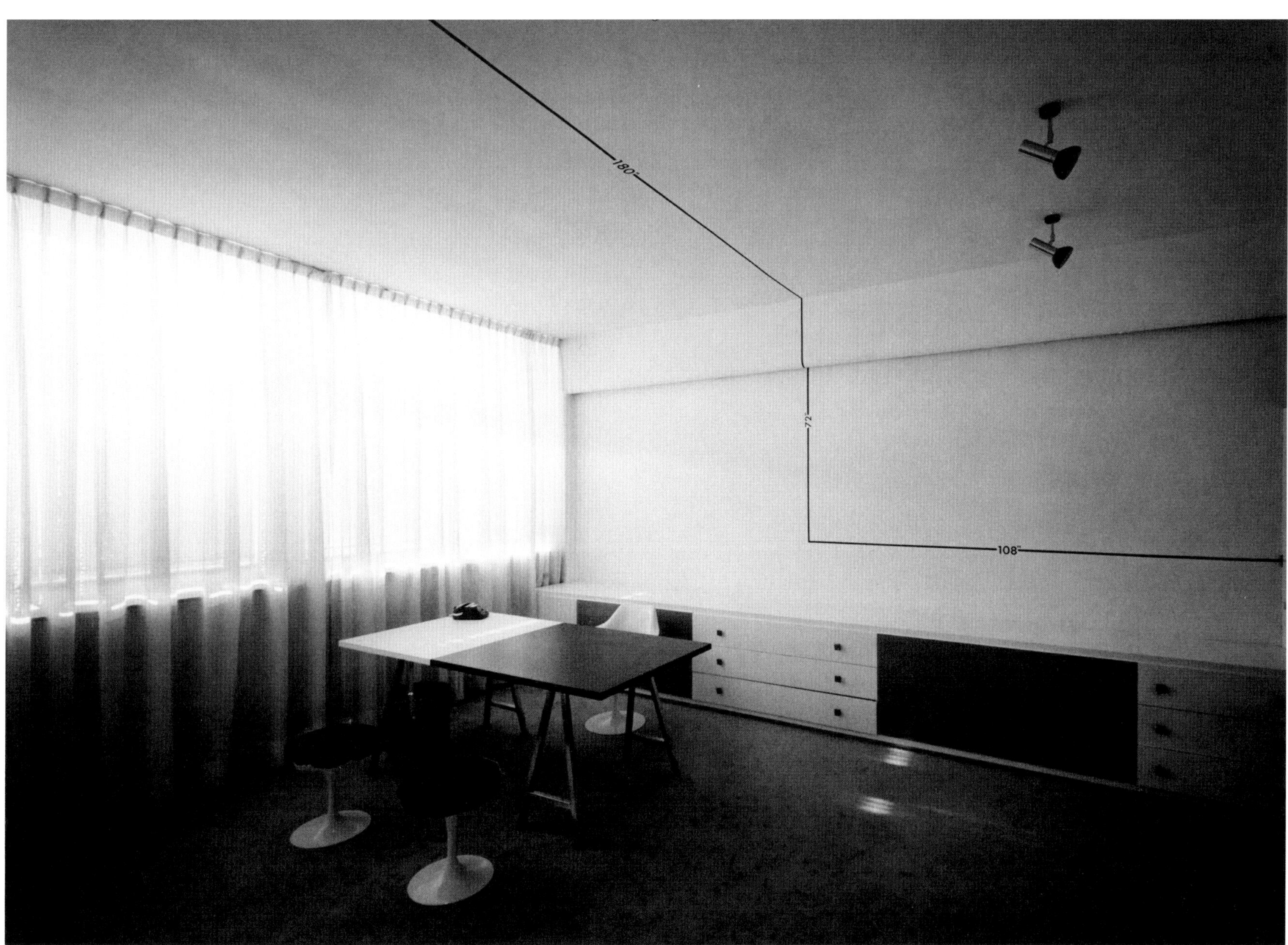
180"
72"
108"

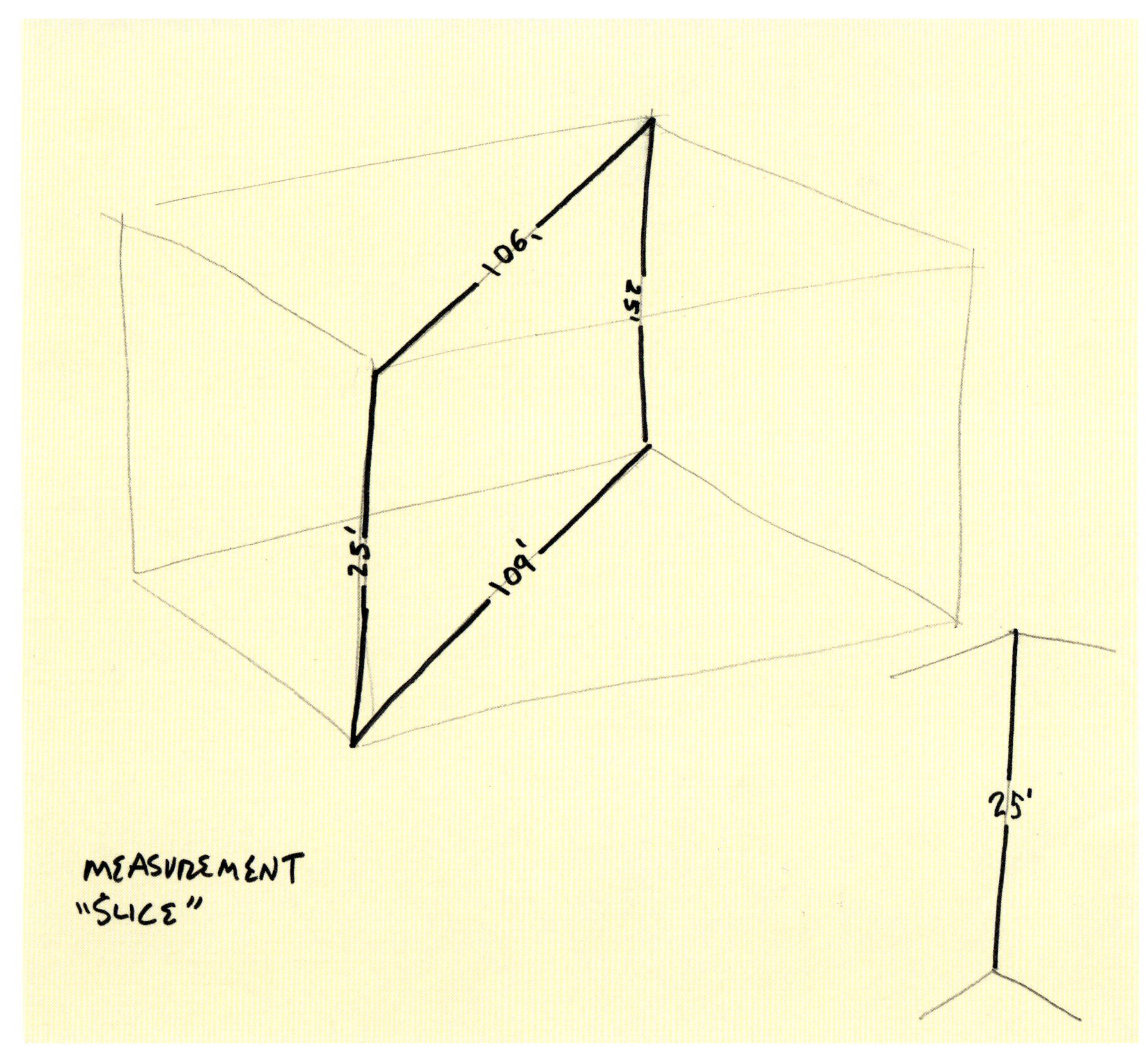

Measurement: Slice, 1969

Ink and pencil on paper

6¾ × 7¼ inches

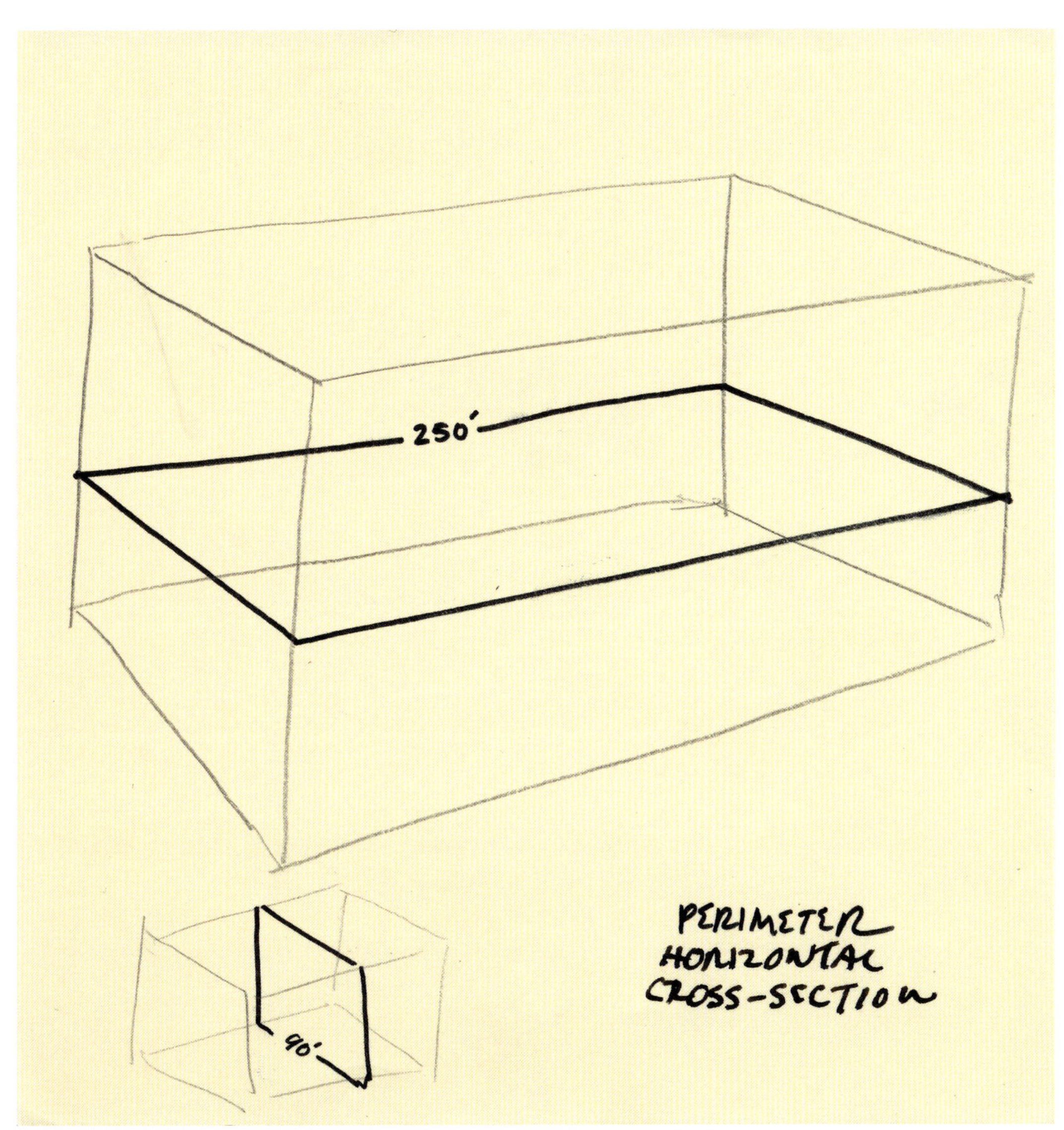

Perimeter Horizontal Cross-Section, 1969

Ink and pencil on paper

7¼ × 6¾ inches

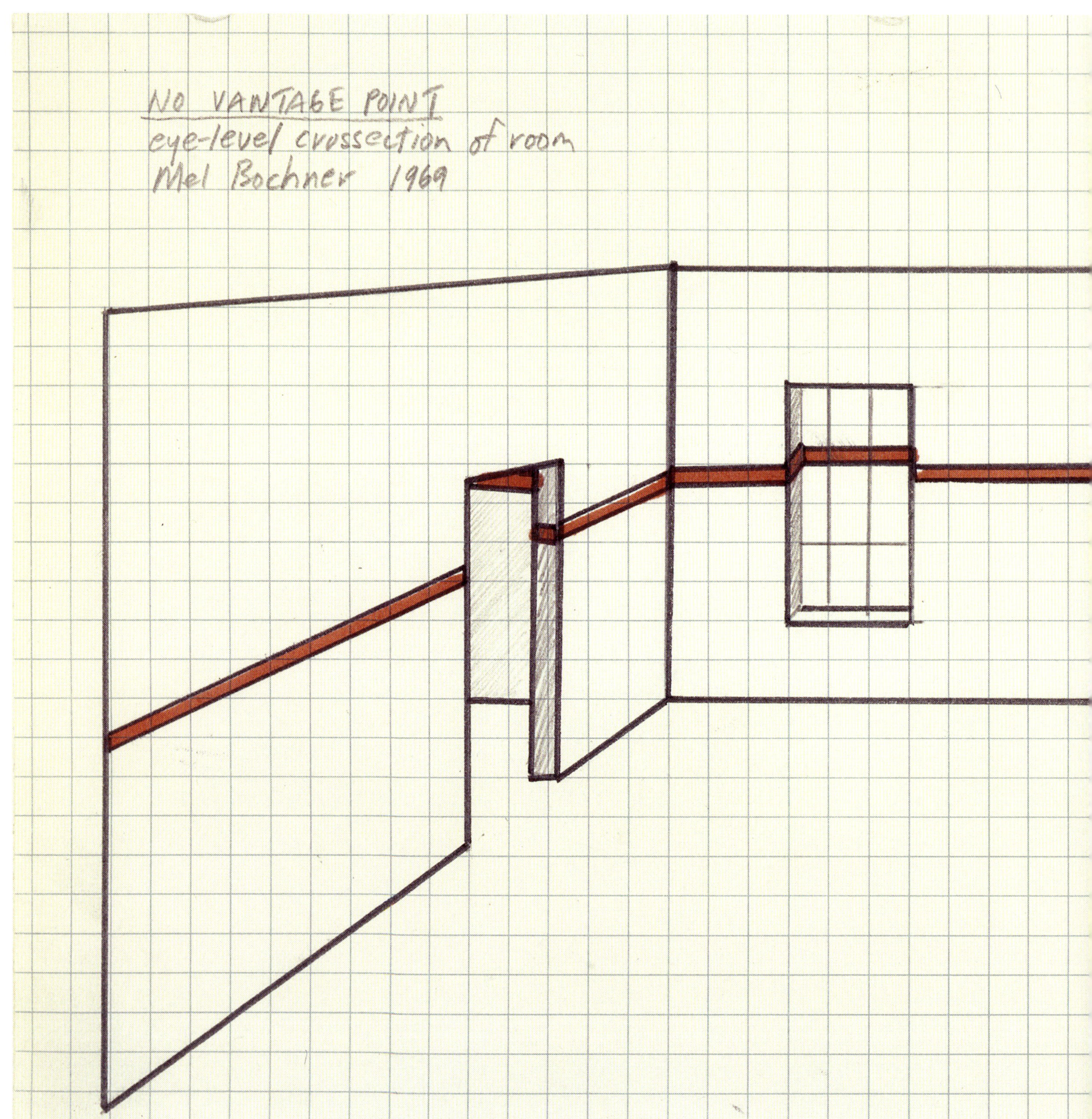
NO VANTAGE POINT
eye-level crossection of room
Mel Bochner 1969

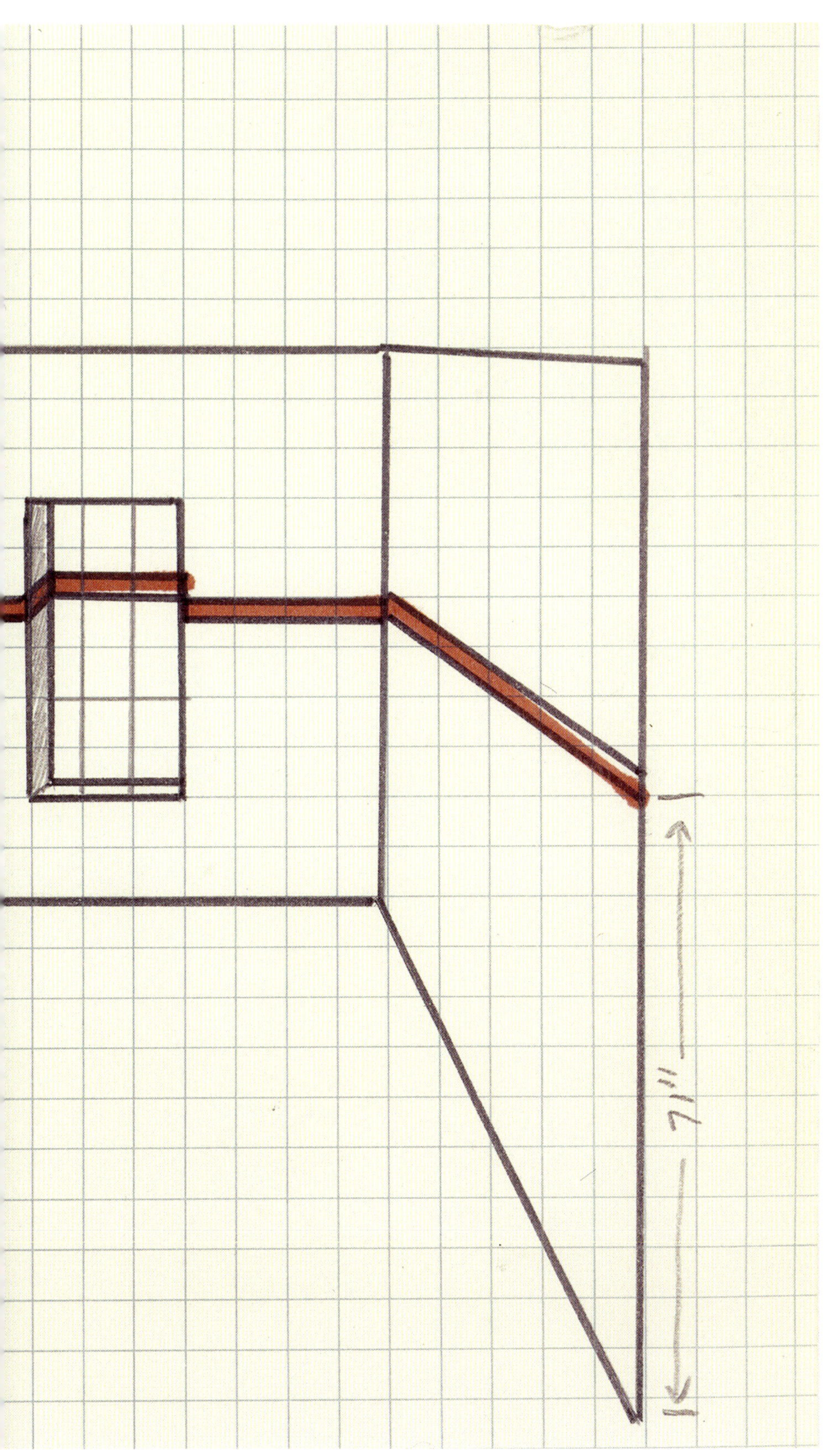

No Vantage Point: Eye Level Cross-Section of a Room, 1969

Ink and pencil on graph paper

7⅛ × 11 inches

Measurement: Shadow, 1969

Ladder, lamp, Letraset, and tape

Installation view, artist's studio, New York

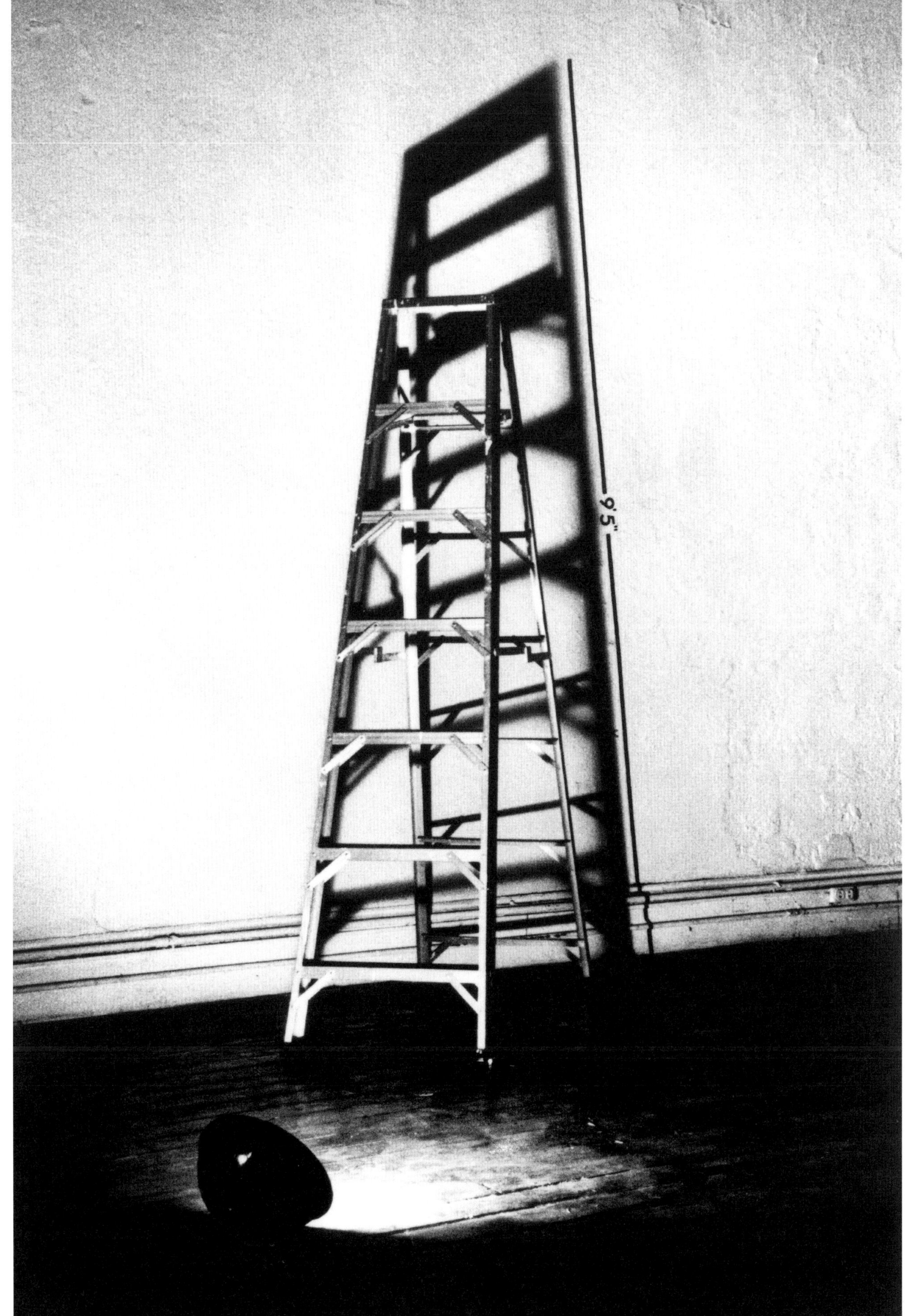
9'5"

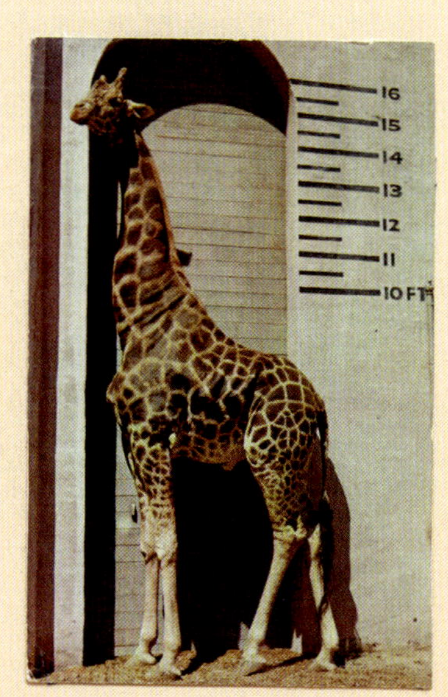

BOCHNER, 1970

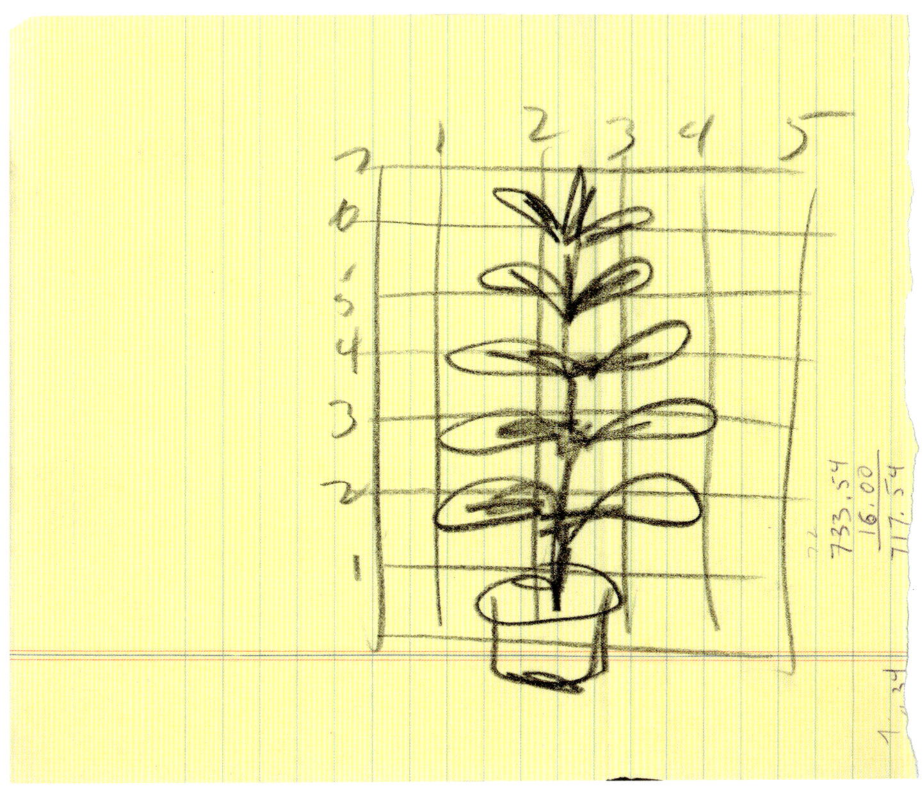

Measurement: Giraffe, 1970
Offset-lithograph postcard on board
16 × 13 inches

Study for Measurement: Plant, 1969
Lithographic pencil on paper
8 × 9¼ inches

Measurement: Plant, 1969

Ficus, tape, and Letraset on wall

Robert Rauschenberg Foundation, New York

Installation view, *Art in Progress IV*, Finch College Museum of Art, New York, 1969

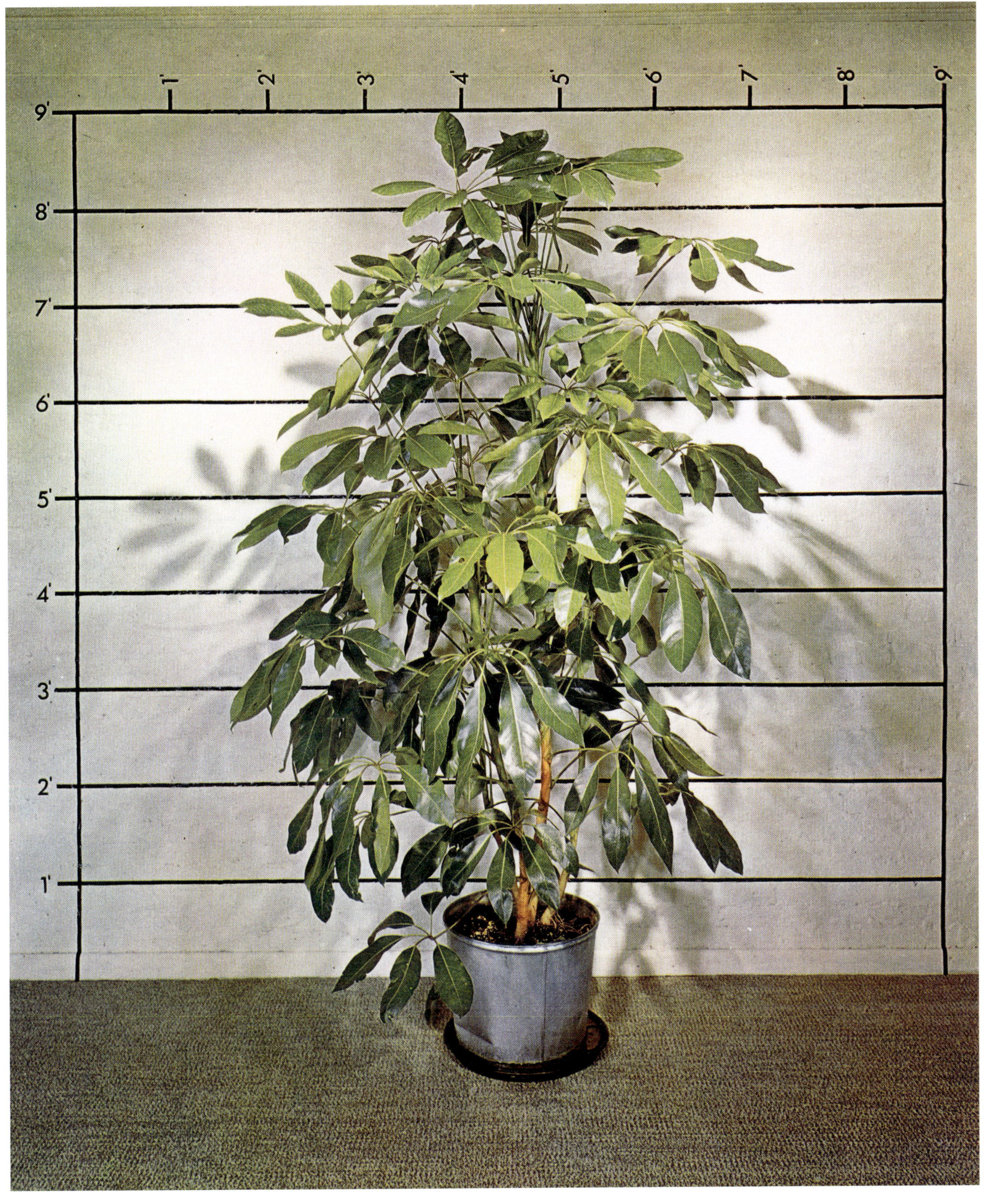
1'
2'
3'
4'
5'
6'
7'
8'
9'
9'
8'
7'
6'
5'
4'
3'
2'
1'

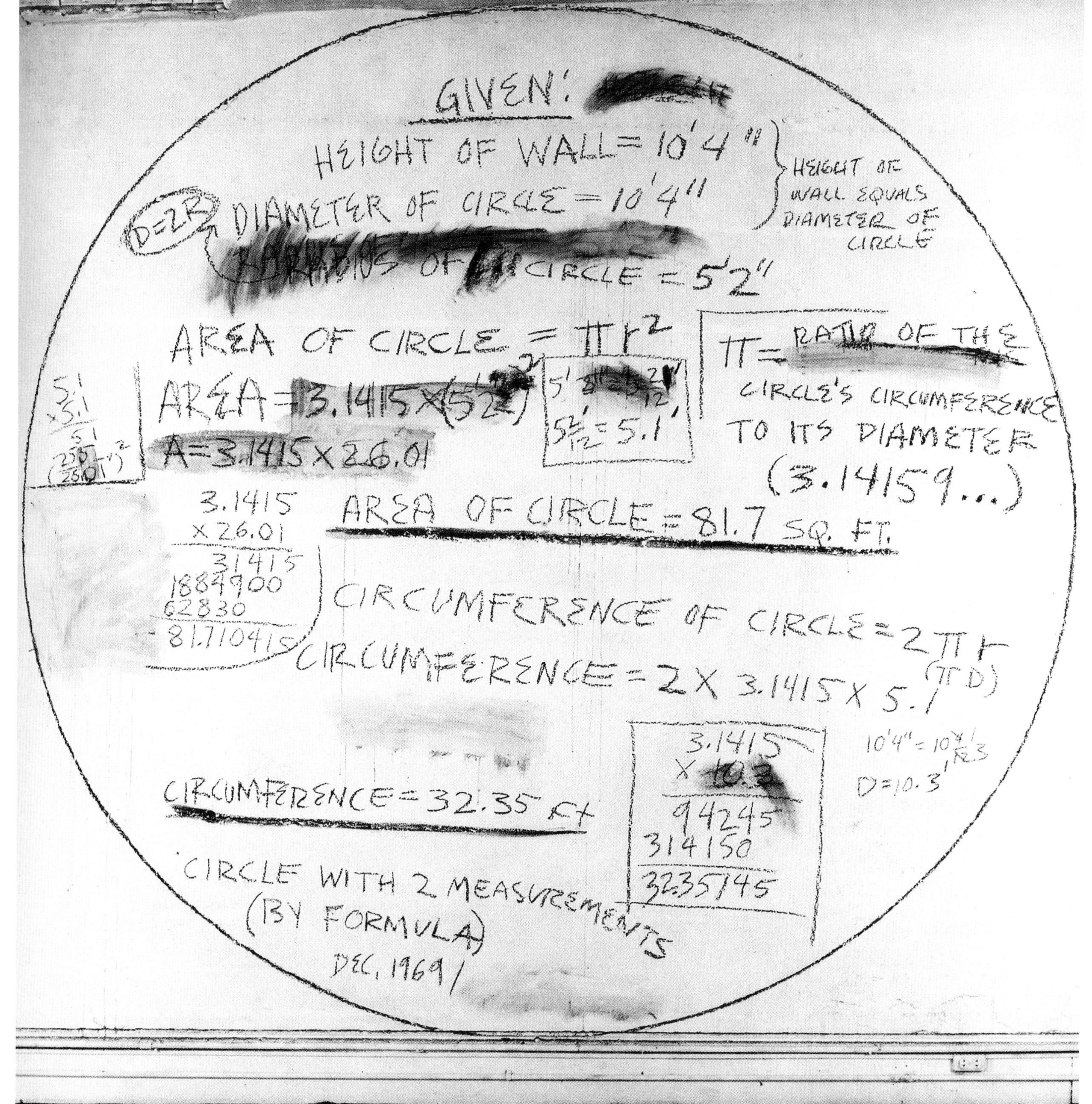
GIVEN:
HEIGHT OF WALL = 10'4"
DIAMETER OF CIRCLE = 10'4"
HEIGHT OF WALL EQUALS DIAMETER OF CIRCLE
D=2R
RADIUS OF CIRCLE = 5'2"
AREA OF CIRCLE = πr²
AREA = 3.1415 X (5'2")²
A = 3.1415 X 26.01
π = RATIO OF THE CIRCLE'S CIRCUMFERENCE TO ITS DIAMETER (3.14159...)
5 2/12 = 5.1'
3.1415
X 26.01
31415
1884900
62830
81.710415
AREA OF CIRCLE = 81.7 SQ. FT.
CIRCUMFERENCE OF CIRCLE = 2πr
(πD)
CIRCUMFERENCE = 2 X 3.1415 X 5.1
3.1415
X 10.3
94245
314150
3235745
D=10.3'
CIRCUMFERENCE = 32.35 FT
CIRCLE WITH 2 MEASUREMENTS
(BY FORMULA)
DEC. 1969

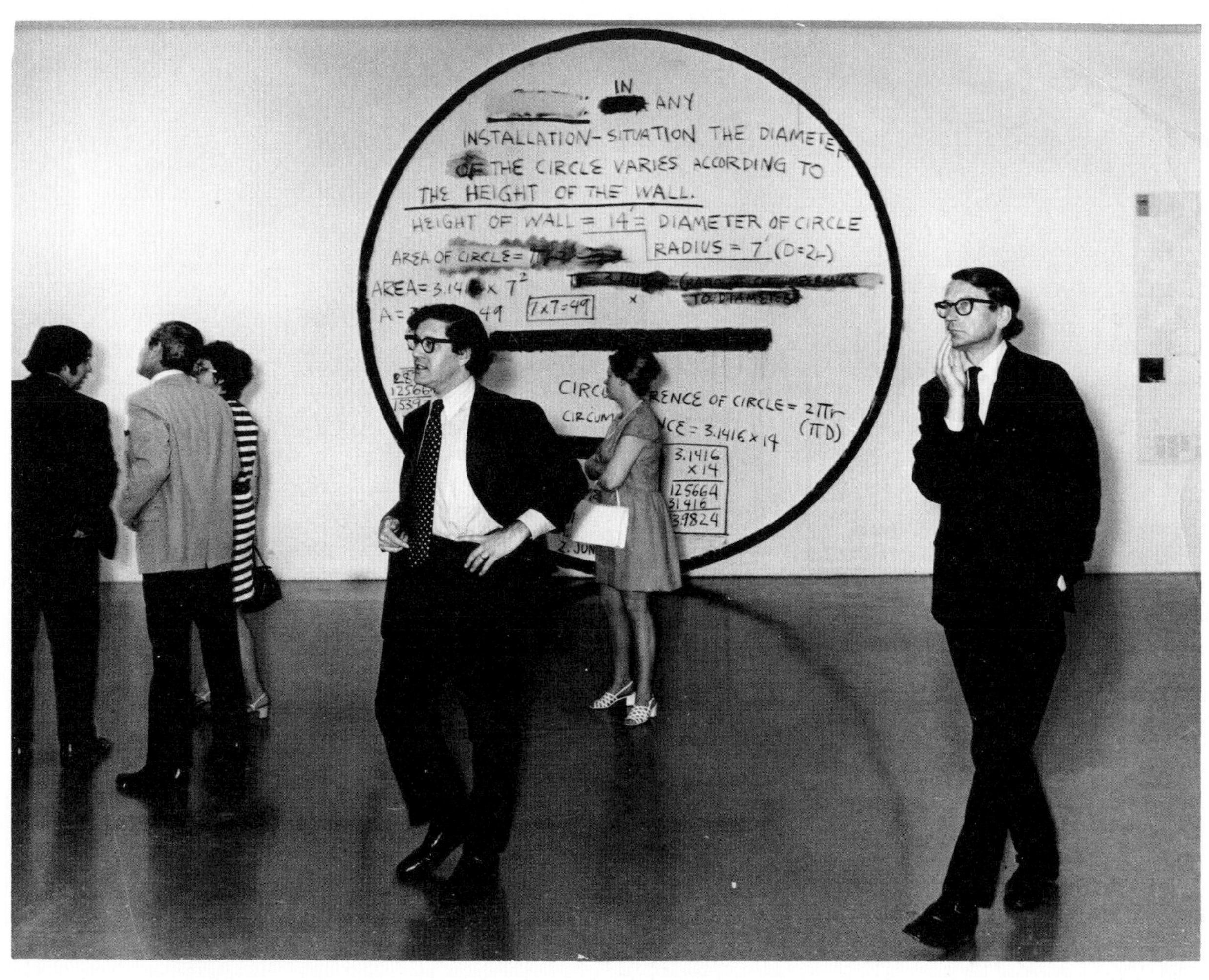

Opposite

Circle with 2 Measurements (By Formula), 1969

Charcoal and paint on wall

Installation view, artist's studio, New York

Above

Installation view, *Information*, Museum of Modern Art, New York, 1970

48 Inches Around the Room, 1969

Pencil and ink on paper

7¼ × 6¾ inches

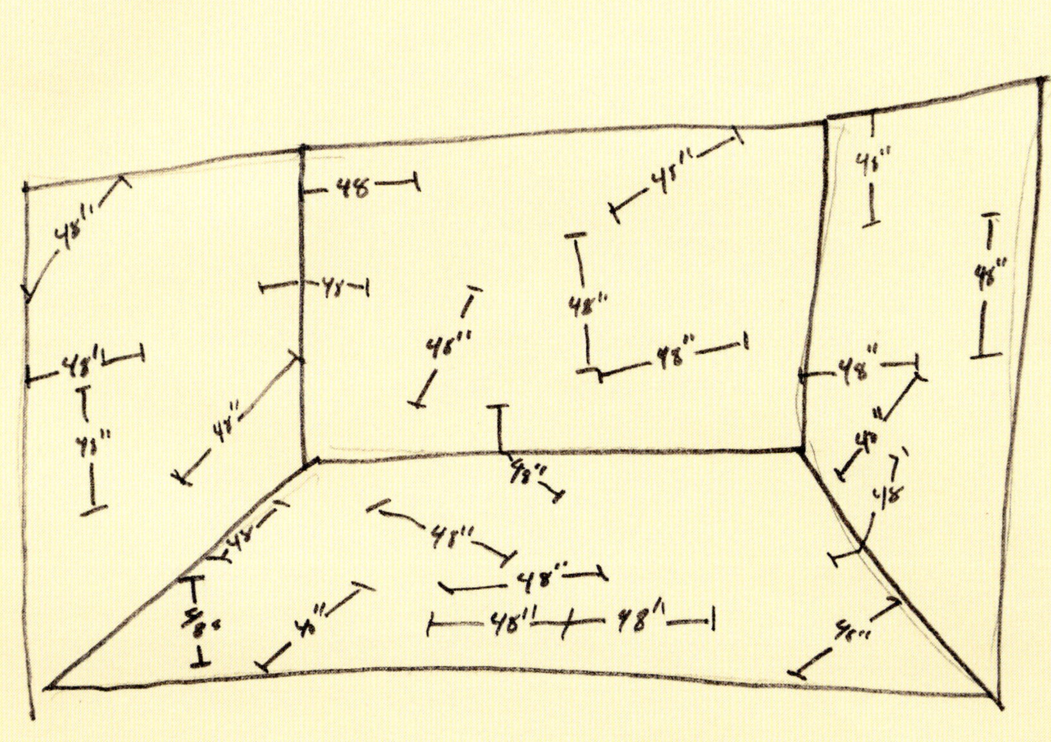

48" around the room

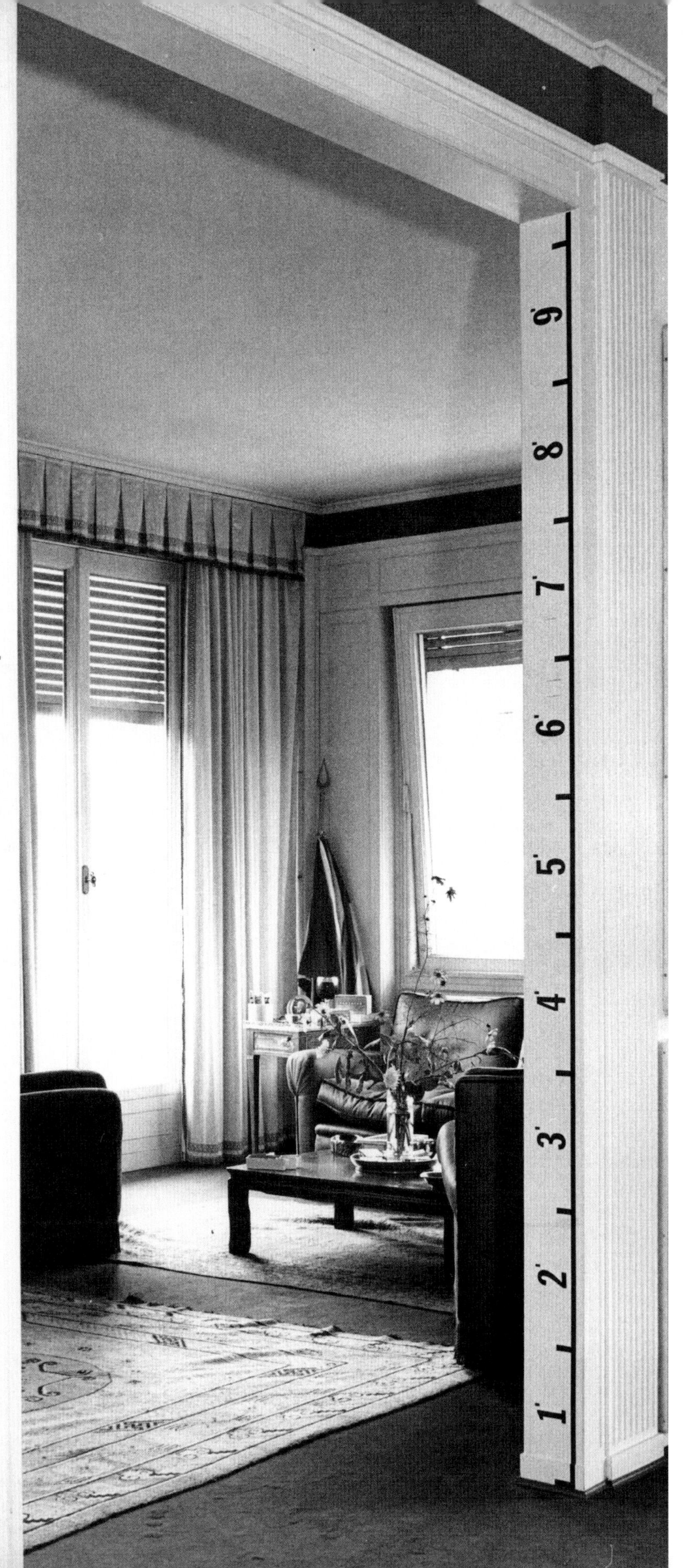

Measurement: Jamb, 1970

Letraset and tape on wall

Installation view, private collection, Milan

Opposite

48 Inches Around the Corner, 1970

Letraset and tape on wall

Installation view, Galleria Sperone, Turin, Italy

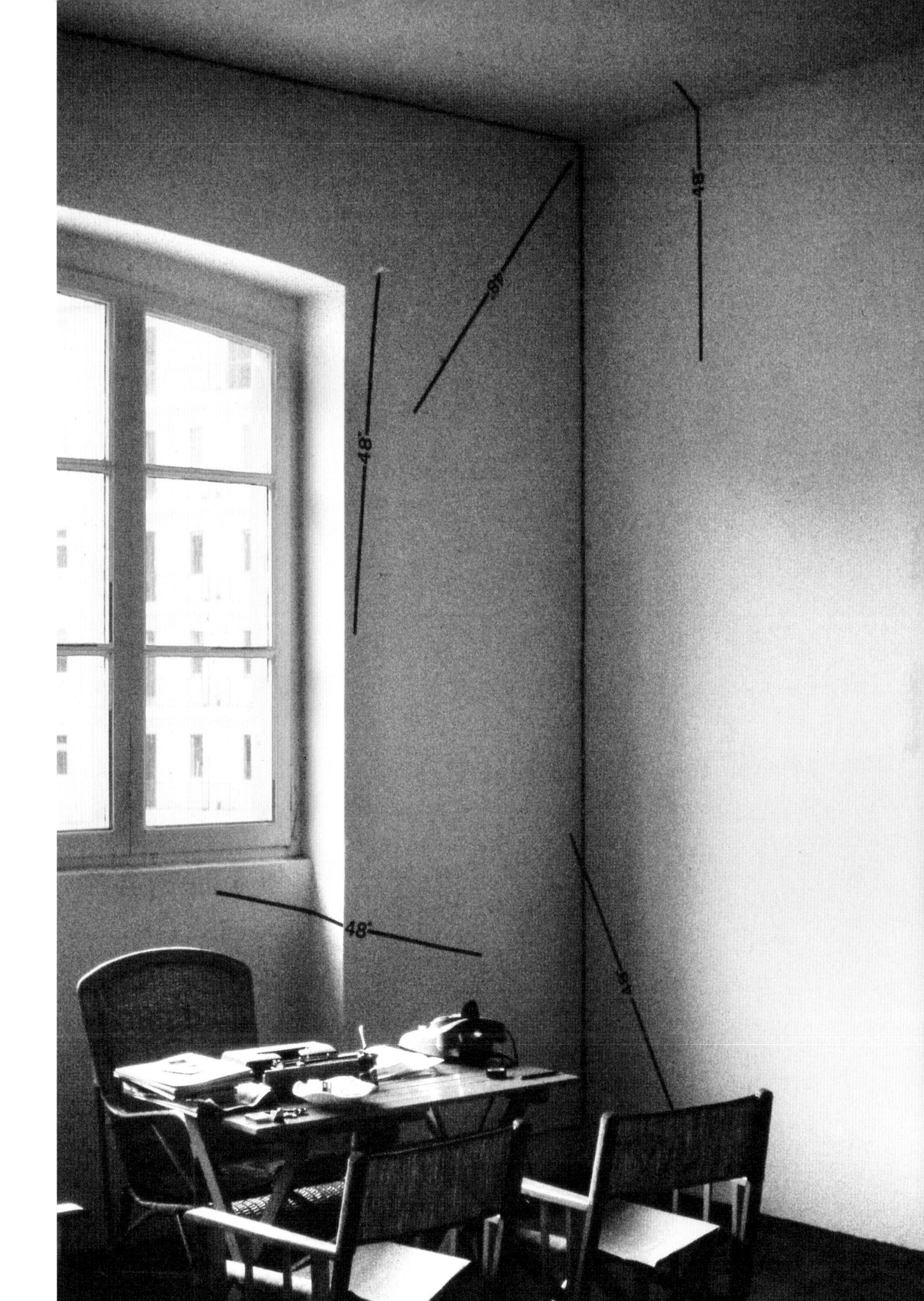

48"
48"
48"

Opposite and following pages

Degrees, 1970

Paint on wall

Installation views, *Degrees*, Galleria Sperone, Turin, Italy, 1970

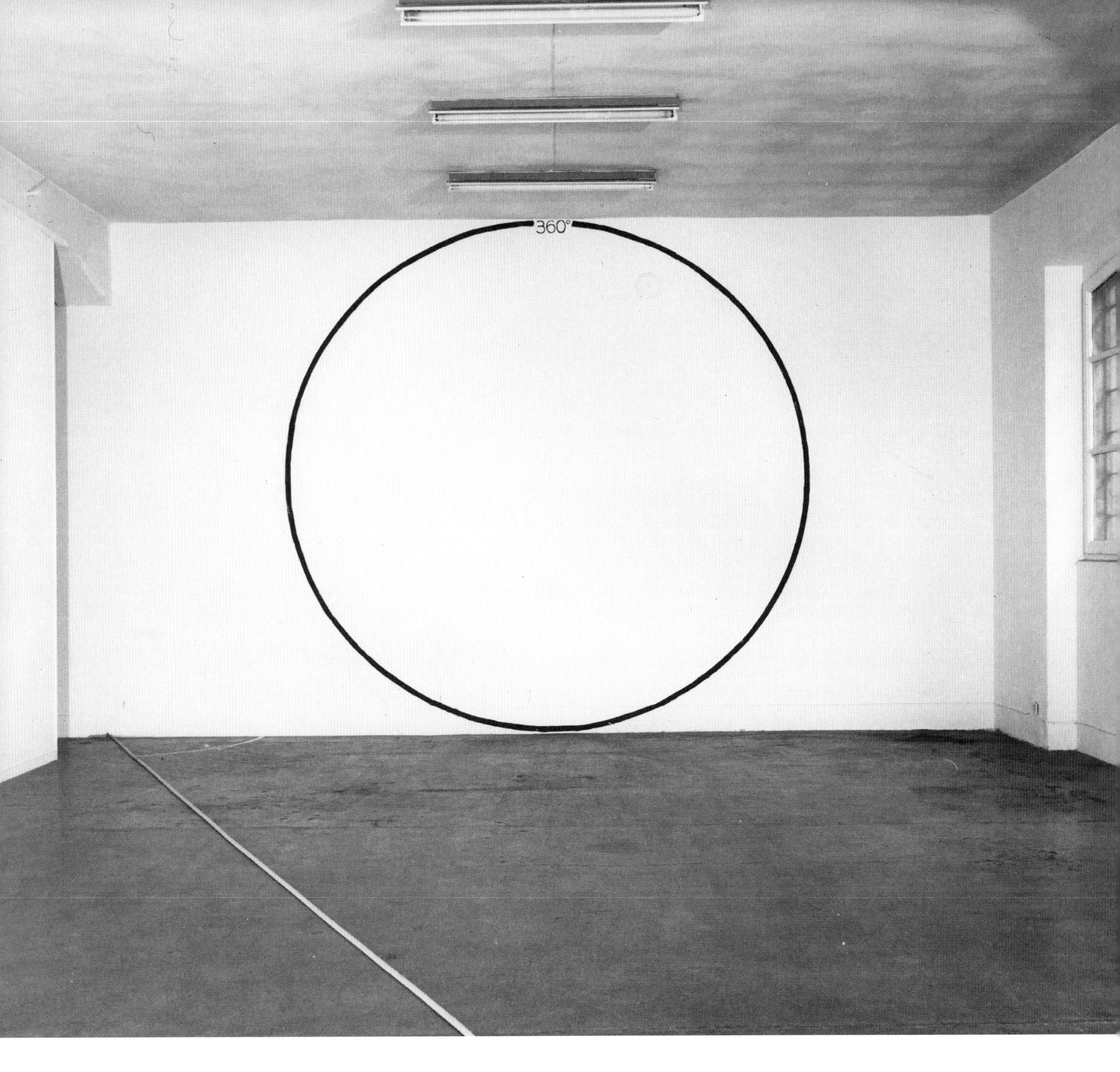
360°

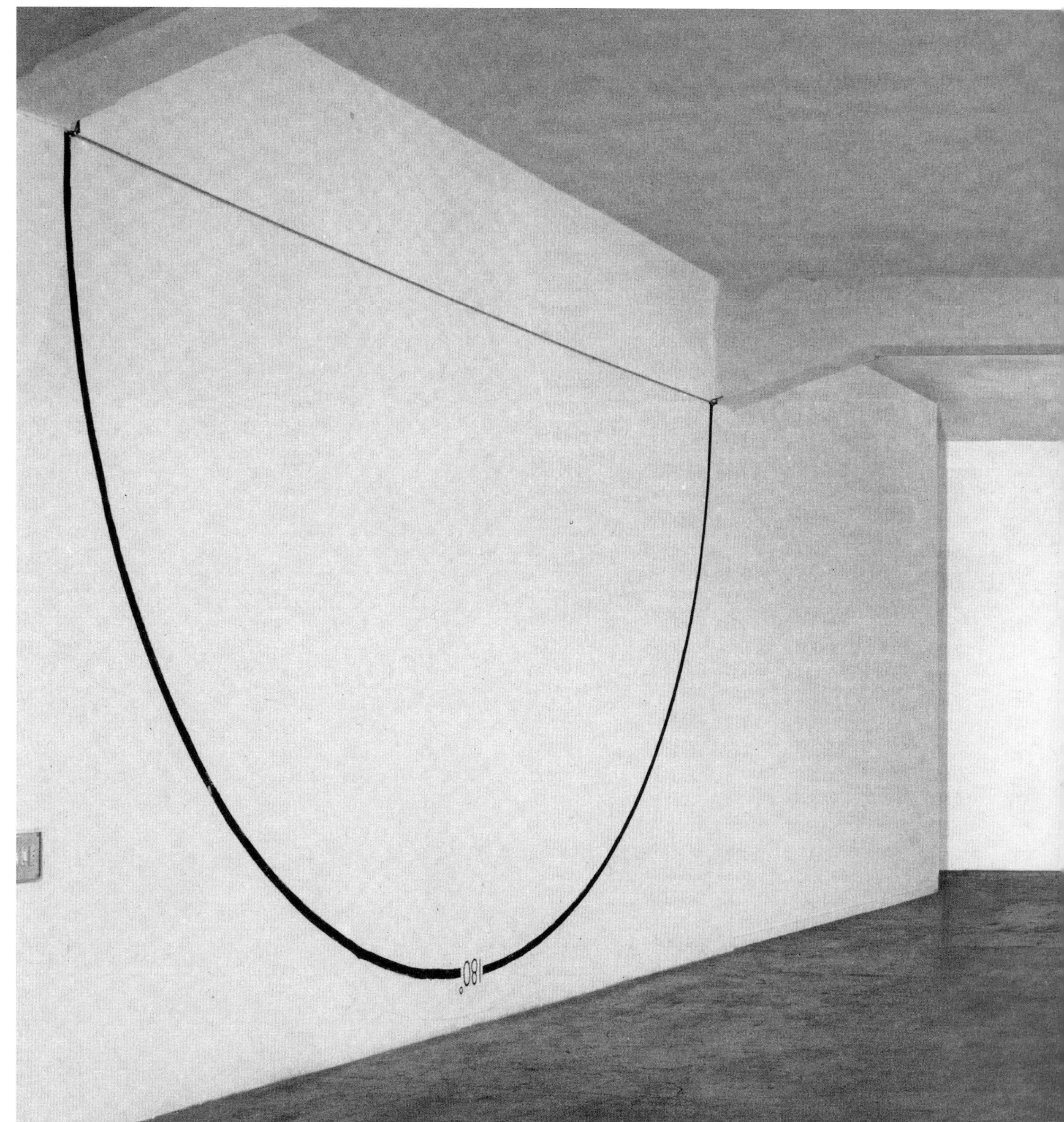

180°

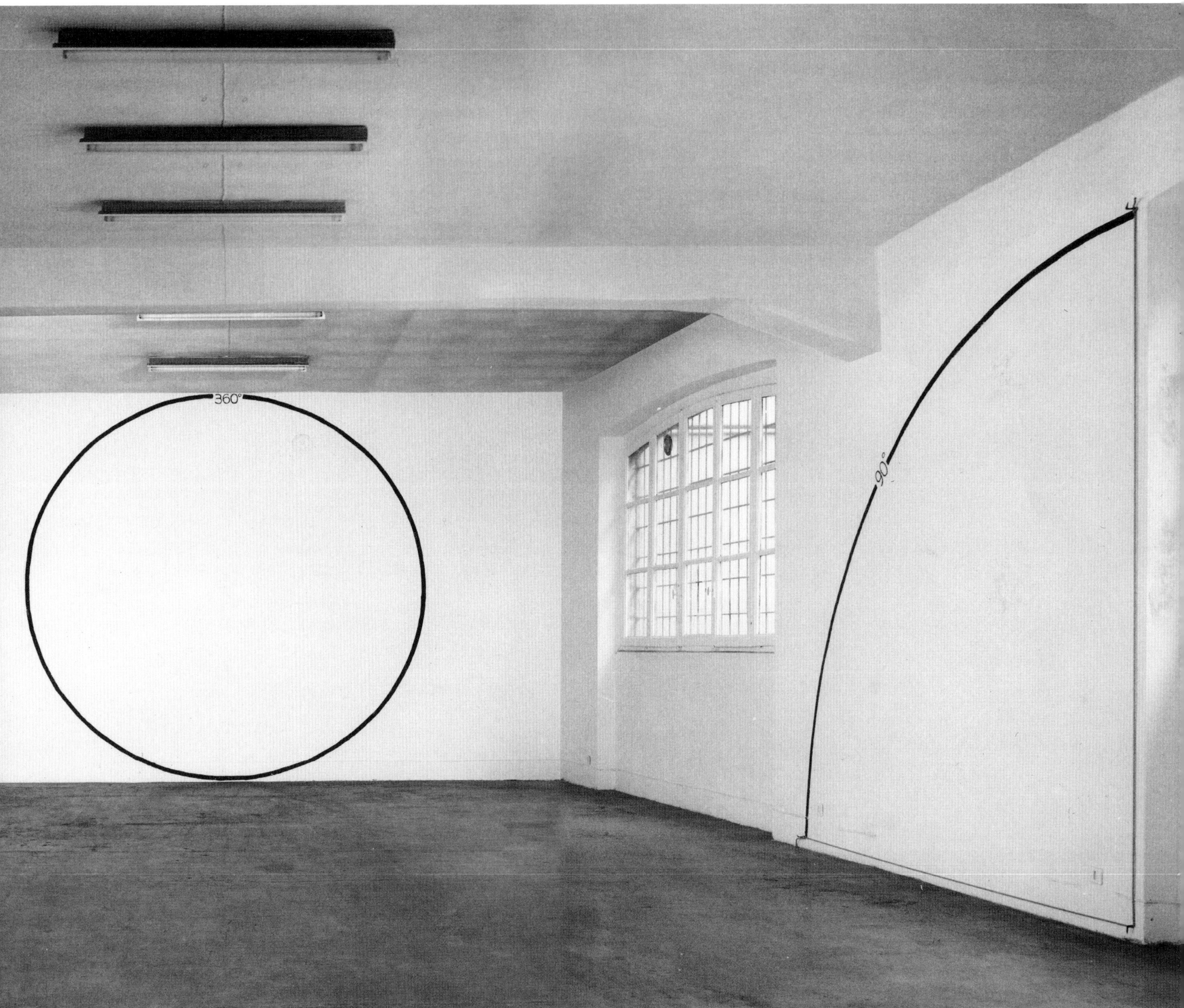

360°
90°

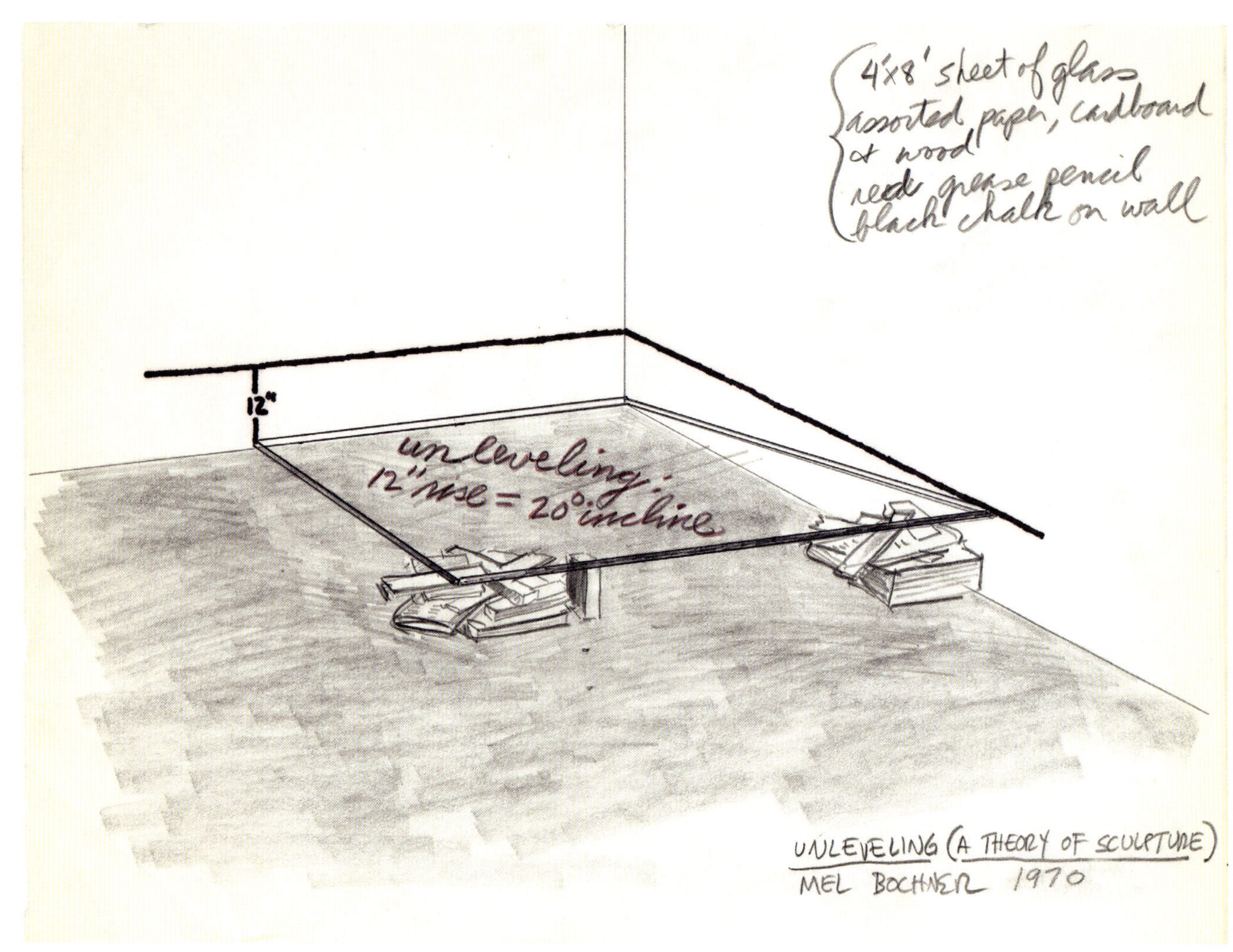

Unleveling (A Theory of Sculpture), 1970

Pencil, ink, and colored pencil on paper

8½ × 11 inches

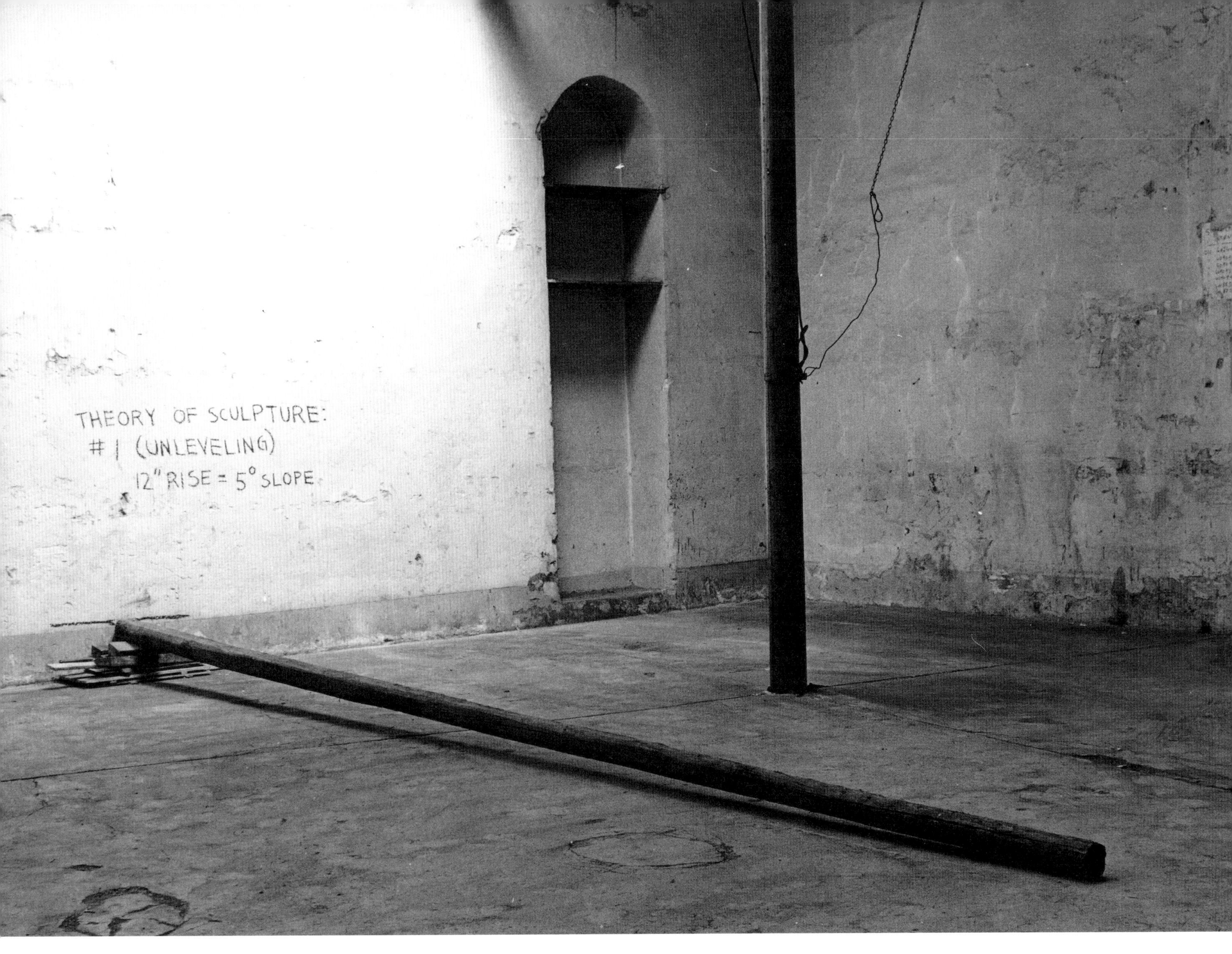

Theory of Sculpture: #1 (Unleveling), 1970

Wood on floor and charcoal on wall

Private collection, Turin, Italy

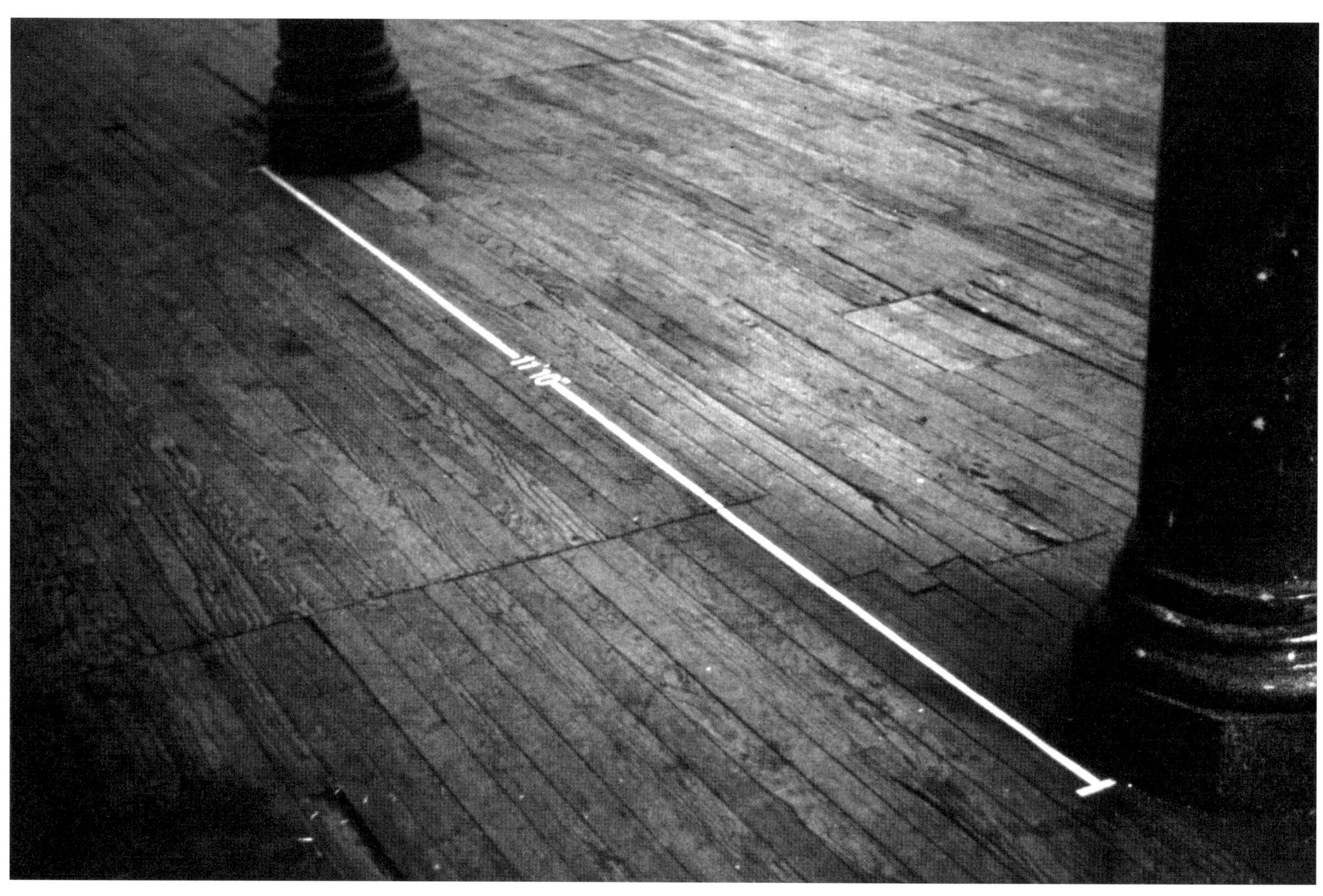

Measurement: Between Columns, 1971

Letraset and tape on floor

Installation view, 112 Greene Street Gallery, New York

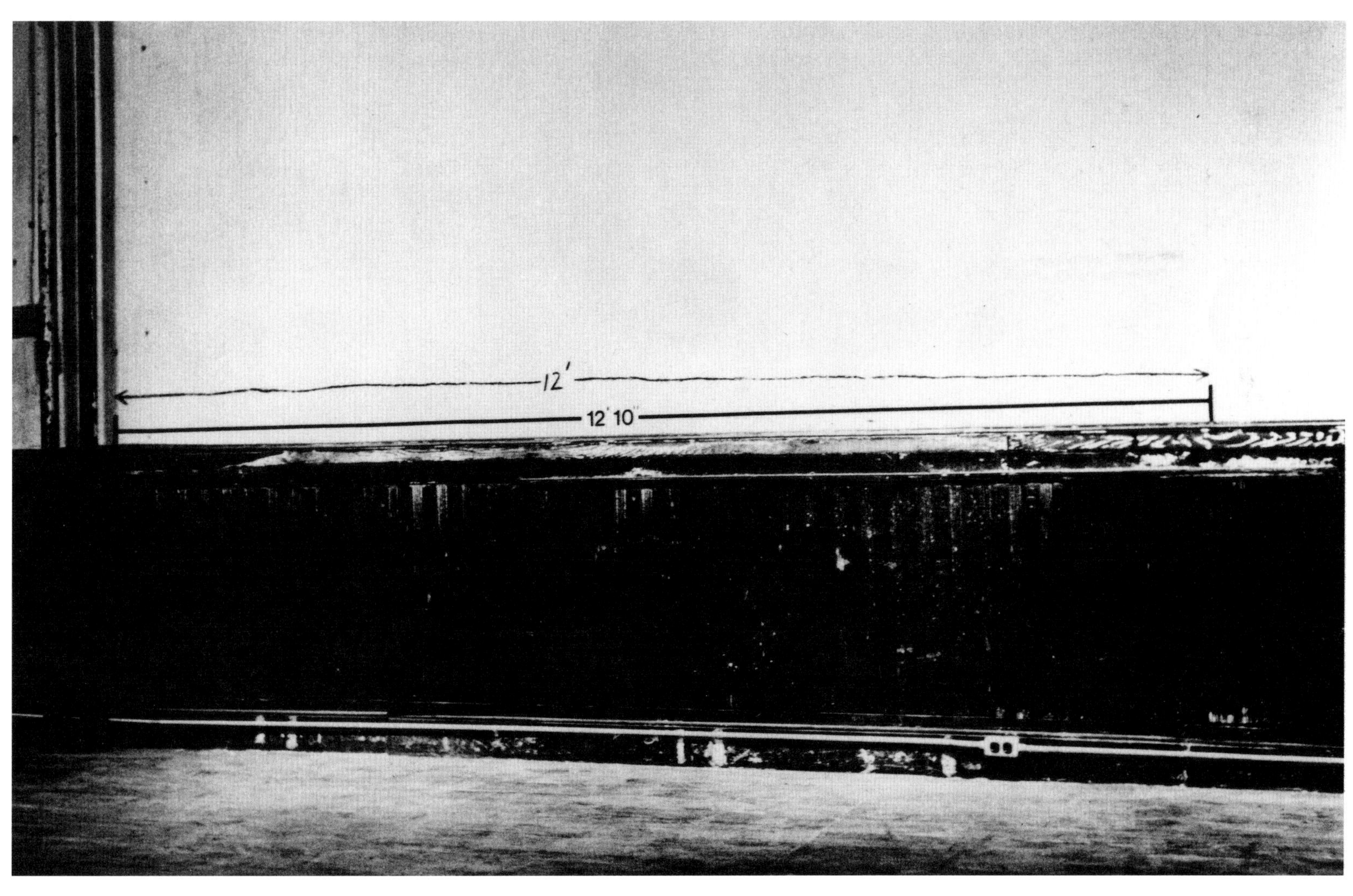

Measurement: Estimated and Measured, 1971
Charcoal, Letraset, and tape on wall
Installation view, 112 Greene Street Gallery, New York

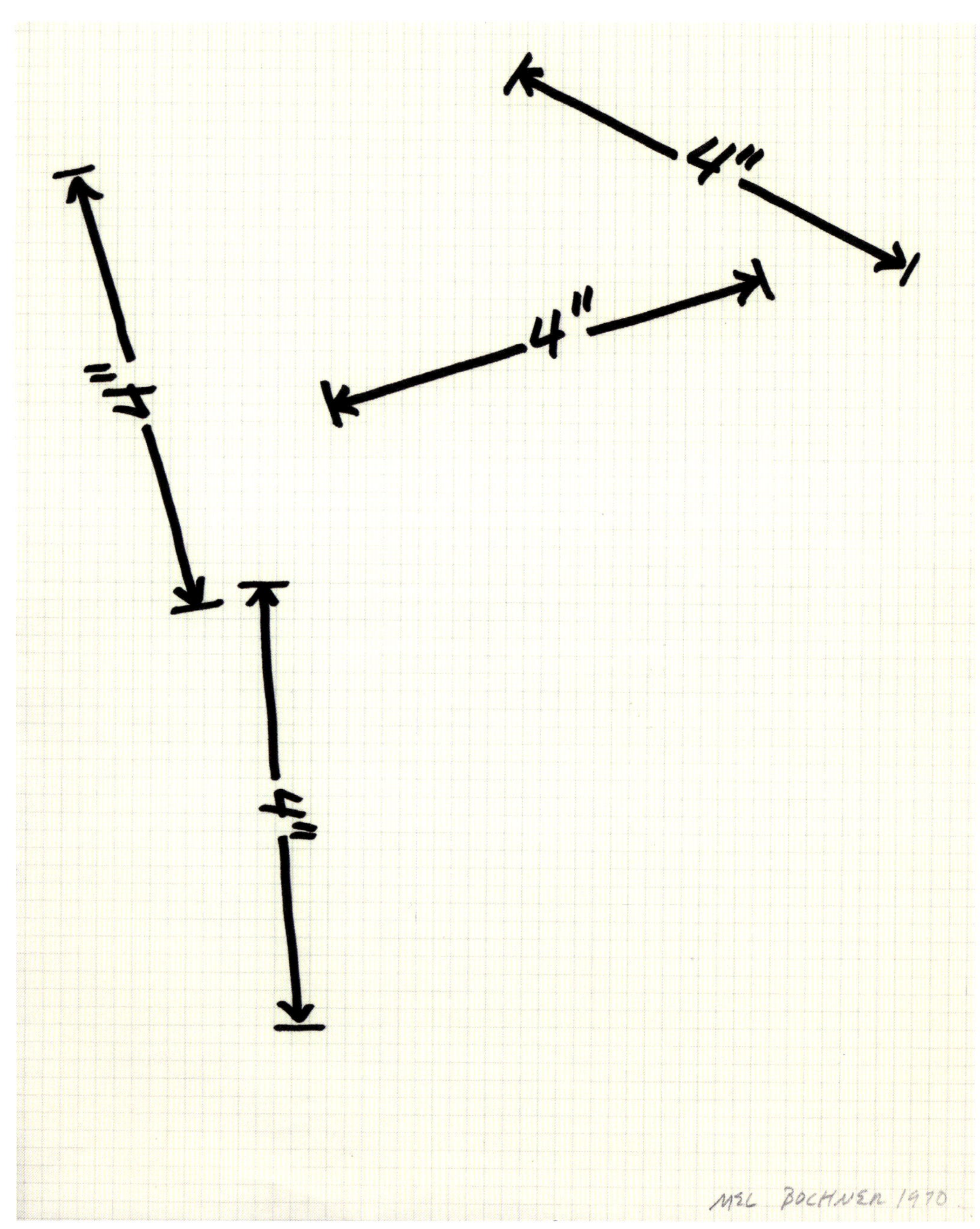

Measurement: 16 Inches, 1970

Ink on graph paper

10¾ × 8⅝ inches

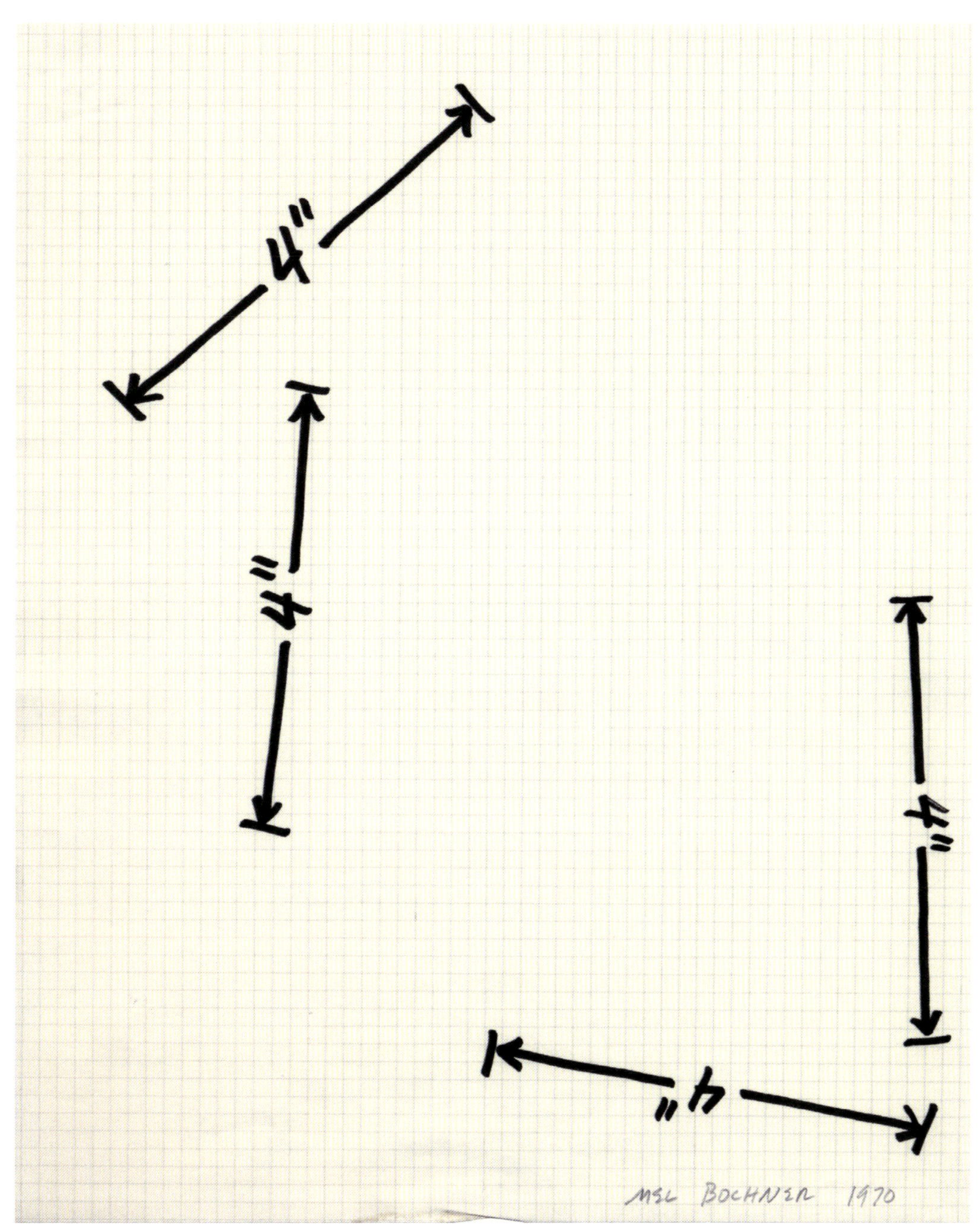

Measurement: 4 Inches Times Four, 1970

Ink on graph paper

10¾ × 8⅝ inches

228

The Museum of Modern Art

11 West 53 Street, New York, N.Y. 10019 Tel. 956-6100 Cable: Modernart

NO. 80
FOR IMMEDIATE RELEASE

PROJECTS: PIER 18

Pier 18, the current exhibition in the series of recent experimental work at The Museum of Modern Art, will be on view through August 2. The exhibition consists of series of photographs by Shunk-Kender, documenting the work of 27 artists on an abandoned pier in the Hudson River last February and March.

The artists were invited to use the pier by Willoughby Sharp, and each work was recorded in photographs upon their instructions. The works take a variety of forms but all relate to the pier. Some artists used the location to carry out an activity or stage an event: Dan Graham was photographed while himself making a series of photographs dictated by shooting with the camera positioned against parts of his body, from the feet to the head. Bill Beckley played 8 notes on a trumpet. Others responded to the physical characteristics of the site itself: George Trakas paddled around the pier in his boat to make drawings of it. In some cases the idea was executed entirely by the photographers, such as Michael Snow's work with simultaneous shots from 2 cameras placed in varying positions, or Jan Dibbet's series from light to dark as the sun goes down.

Other artists in the exhibition are: Vito Acconci, David Askevold, John Baldessari, Robert Barry, Mel Bochner, Daniel Buren, Terry Fox, Douglas Huebler, Lee Jaffe, Richards Jarden, Gordon Matta, Mario Merz, Robert Morris, Dennis Oppenheim, Allen Ruppersberg, Italo Scanga, Richard Serra, Keith Sonnier, Wolfgang Stoerchle, John Van Saun, William Wegman and Lawrence Weiner.

The exhibition was installed by Jennifer Licht, Associate Curator, Department of Painting and Sculpture.

* *

Additional information available from Elizabeth Shaw, Director, Department of Public Information, The Museum of Modern Art, 11 W. 53 St., New York, N.Y. 10019. Phone: (212) 956-7501.

July 1971

Press release for *Pier 18*, Museum of Modern Art, New York, 1971

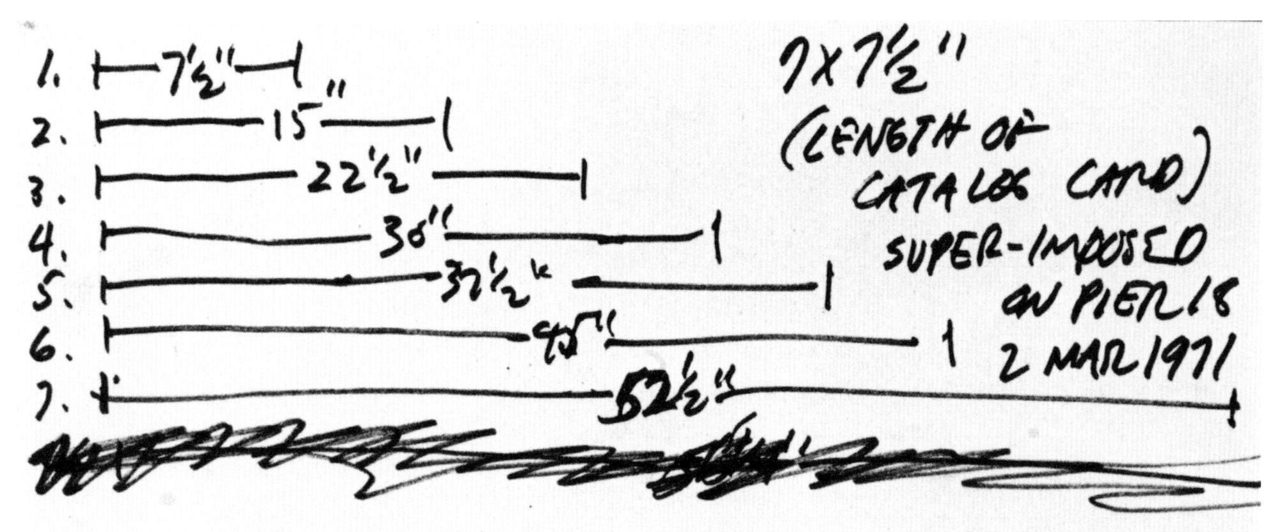

7 × 7½ Inches, 1971

Ink on paper

5 × 8 inches

Opposite and following pages

Project for Pier 18, 1971

Chalk on various surfaces

Installation view, Pier 18, New York

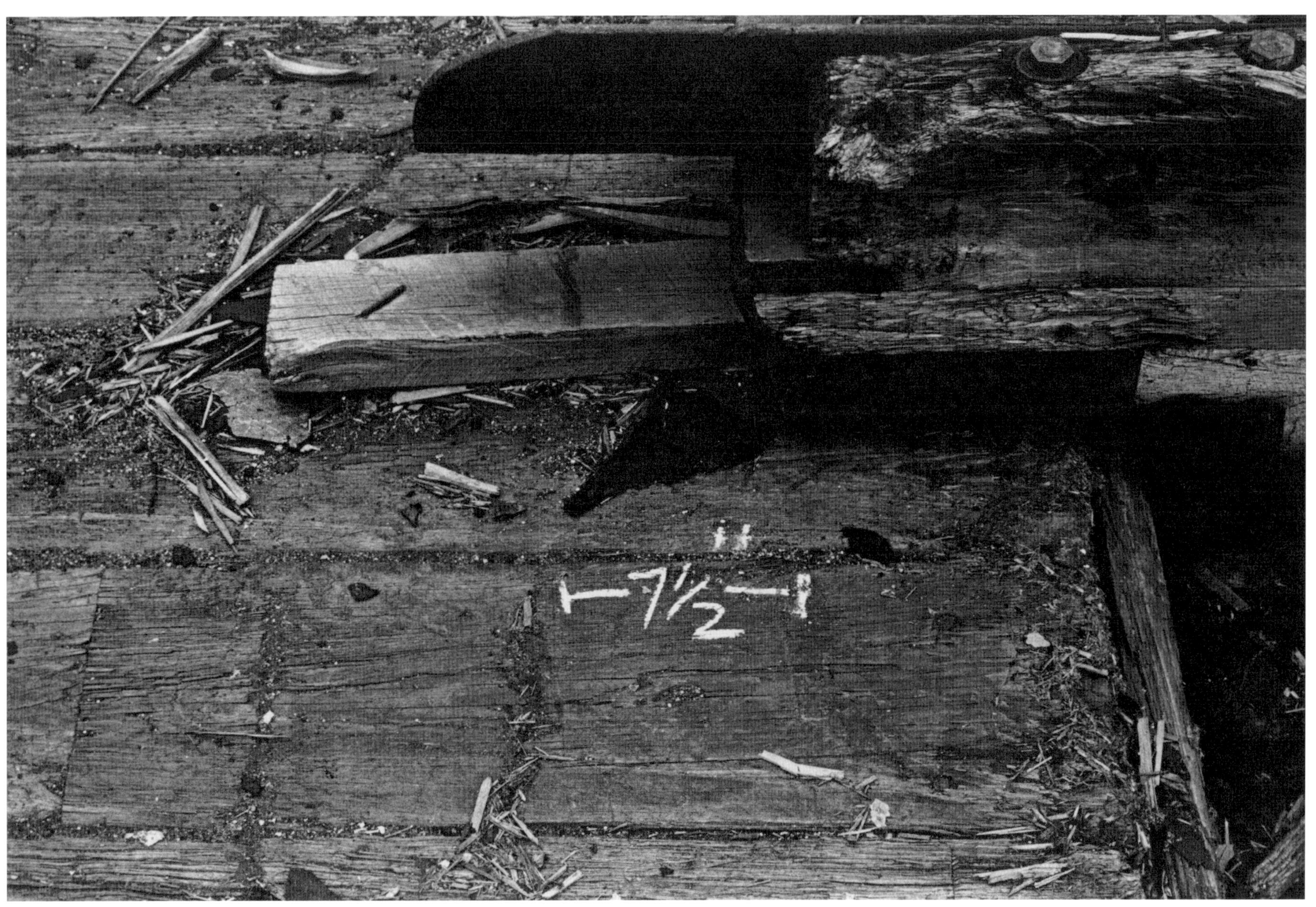
7½"

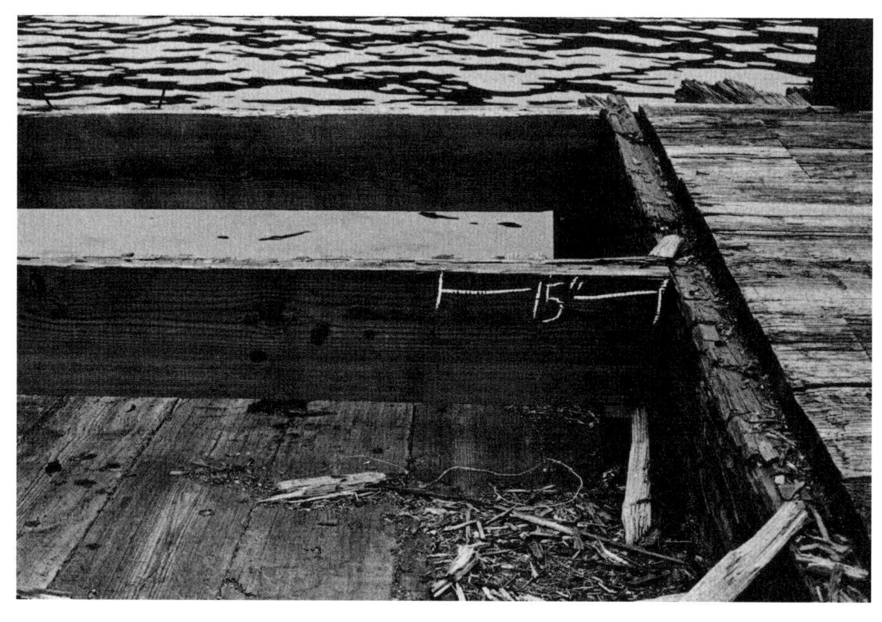
15"

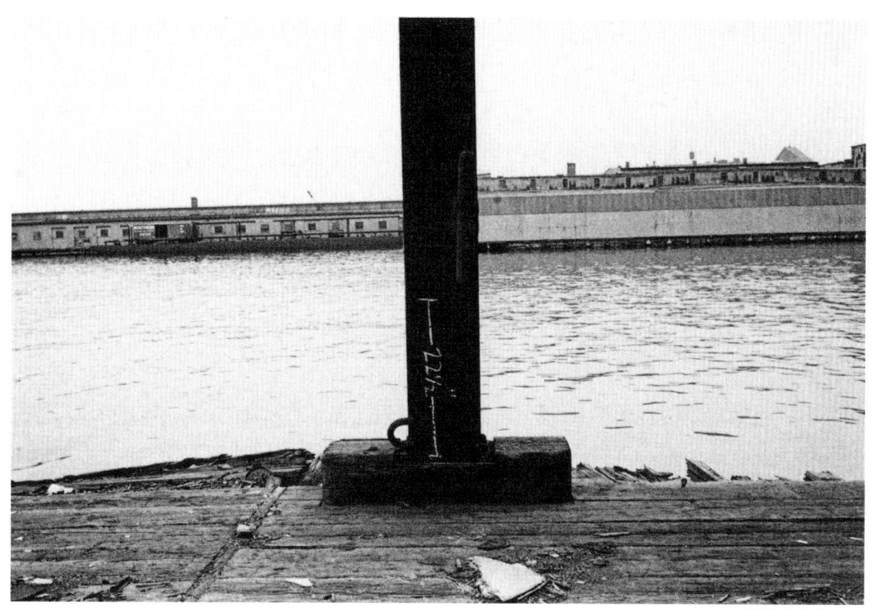

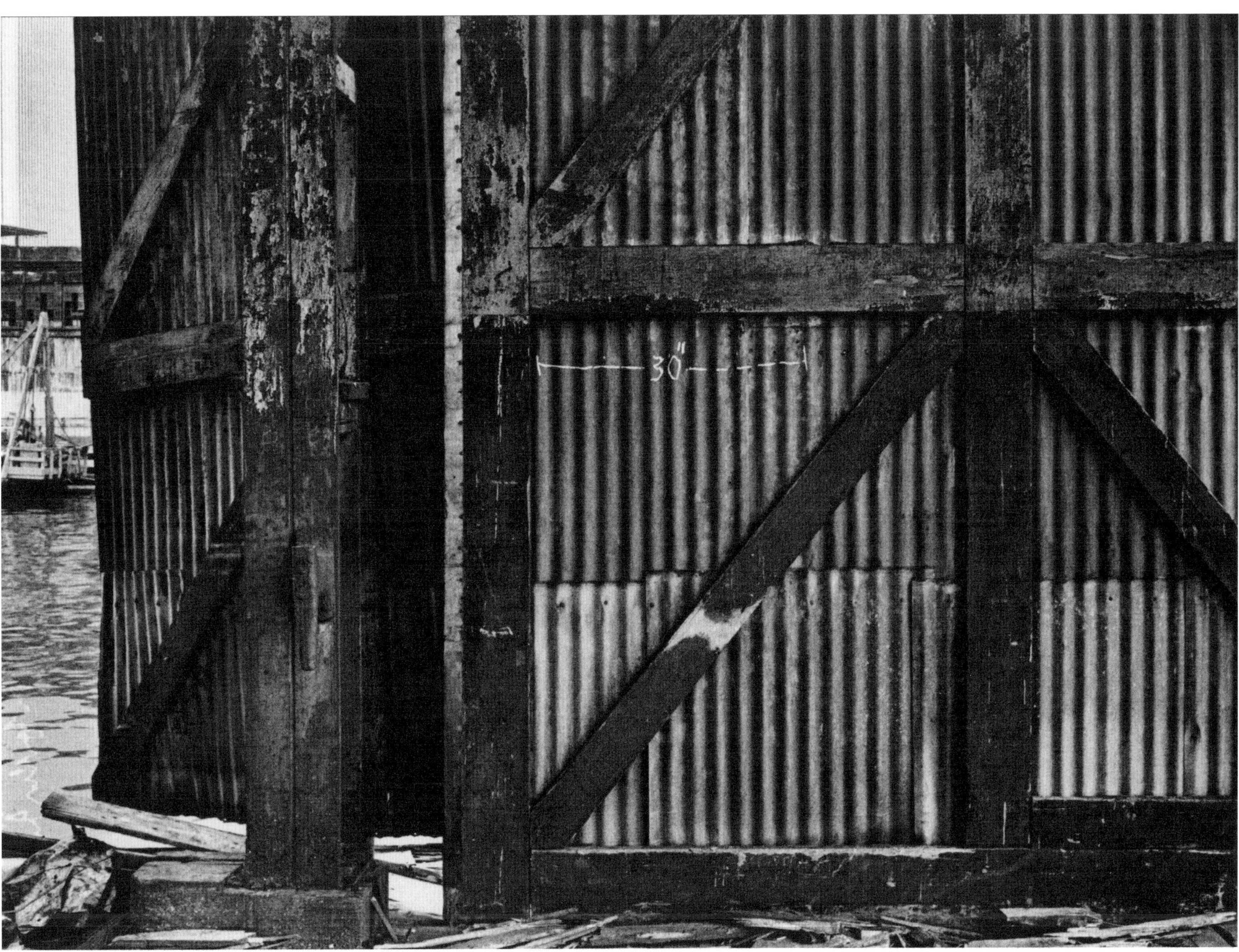
30"

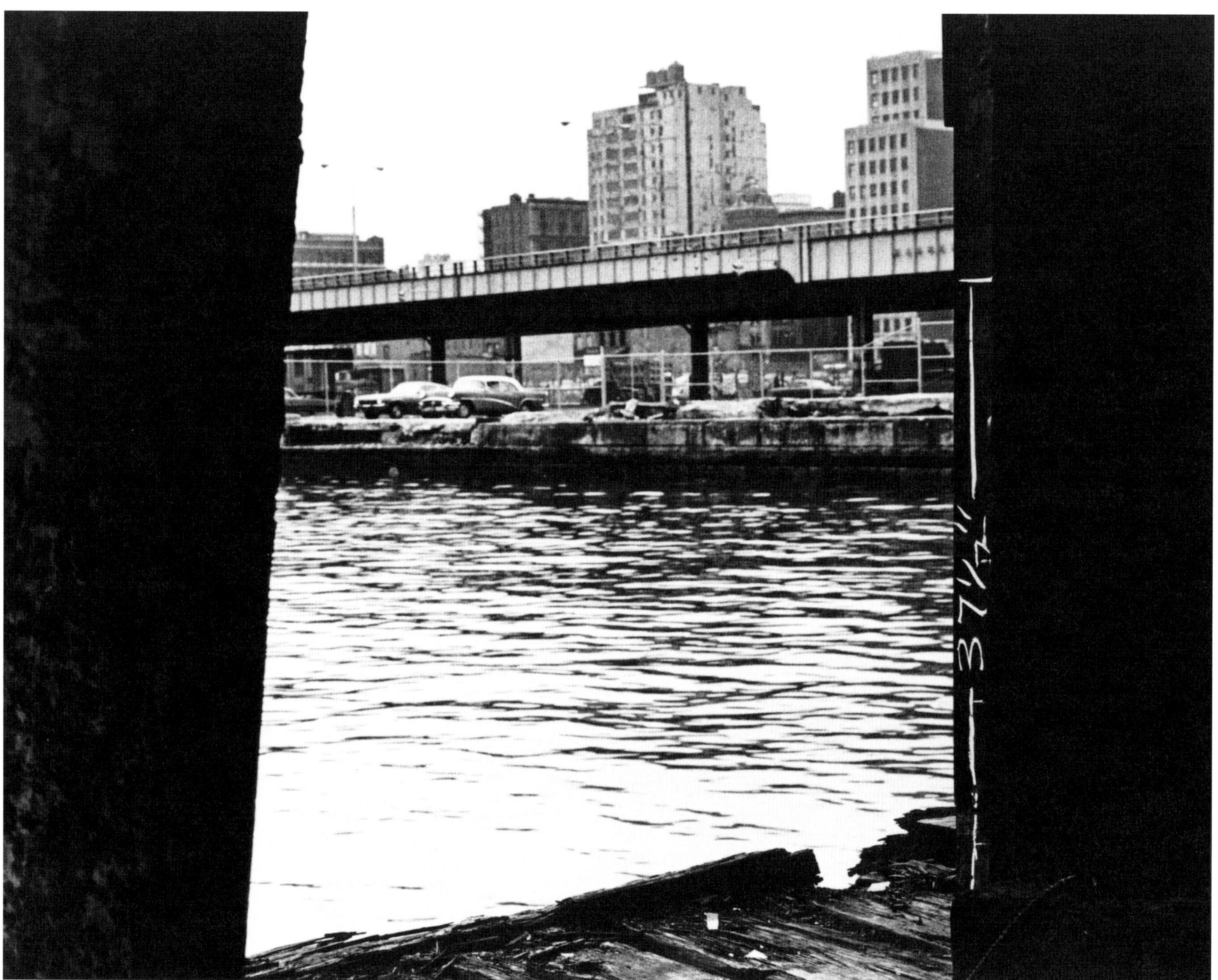
37½″

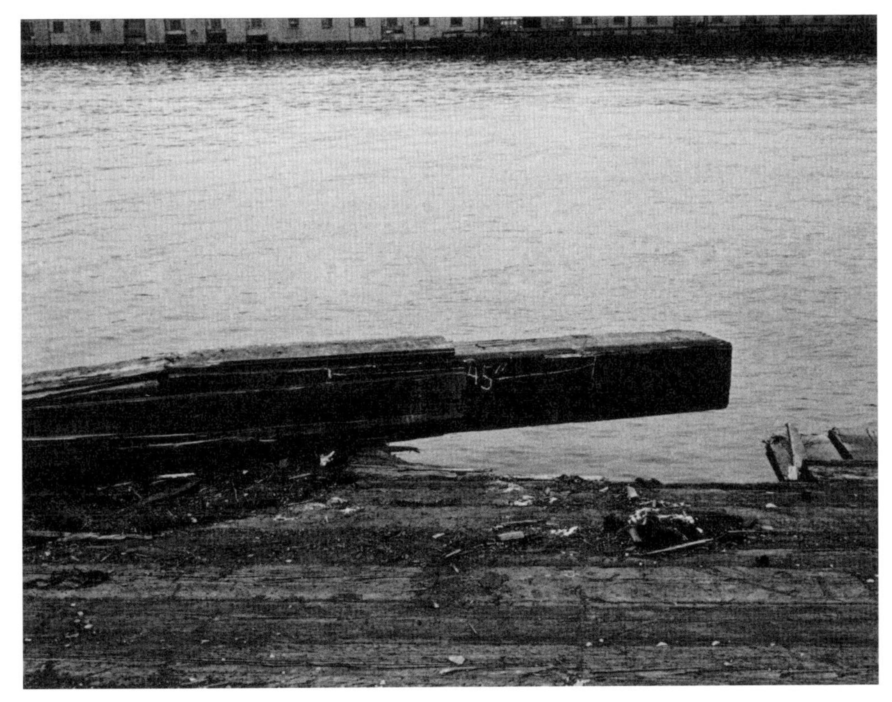
45"

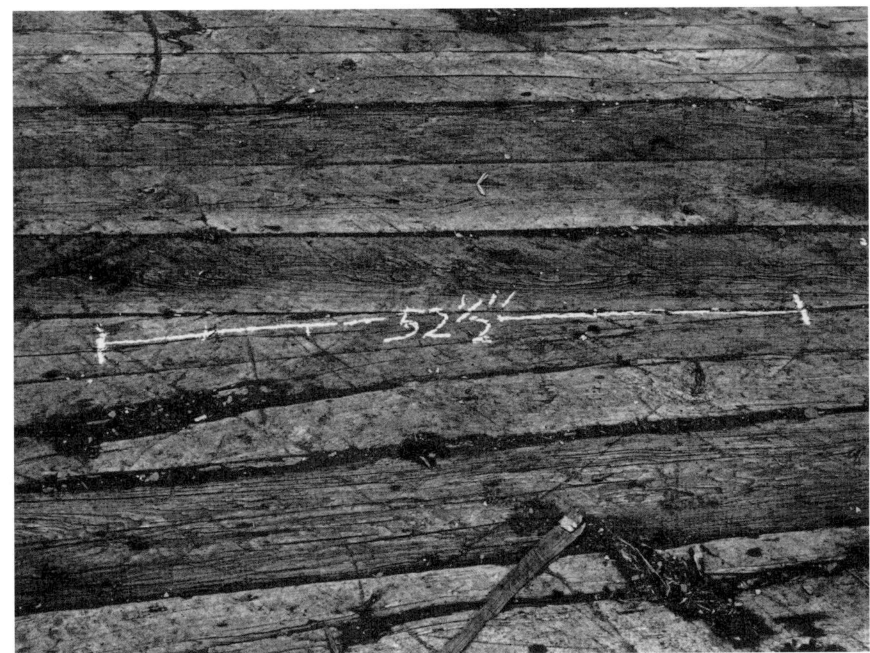
52½"

Measurement – From the Space of Statements, 1969
Vinyl on wall (with Piet Mondrian, *Fox Trot B*, 1929)
Installation view, *Mel Bochner: Thought Made Visible, 1966–1973,*
Yale University Art Gallery, New Haven, 1995

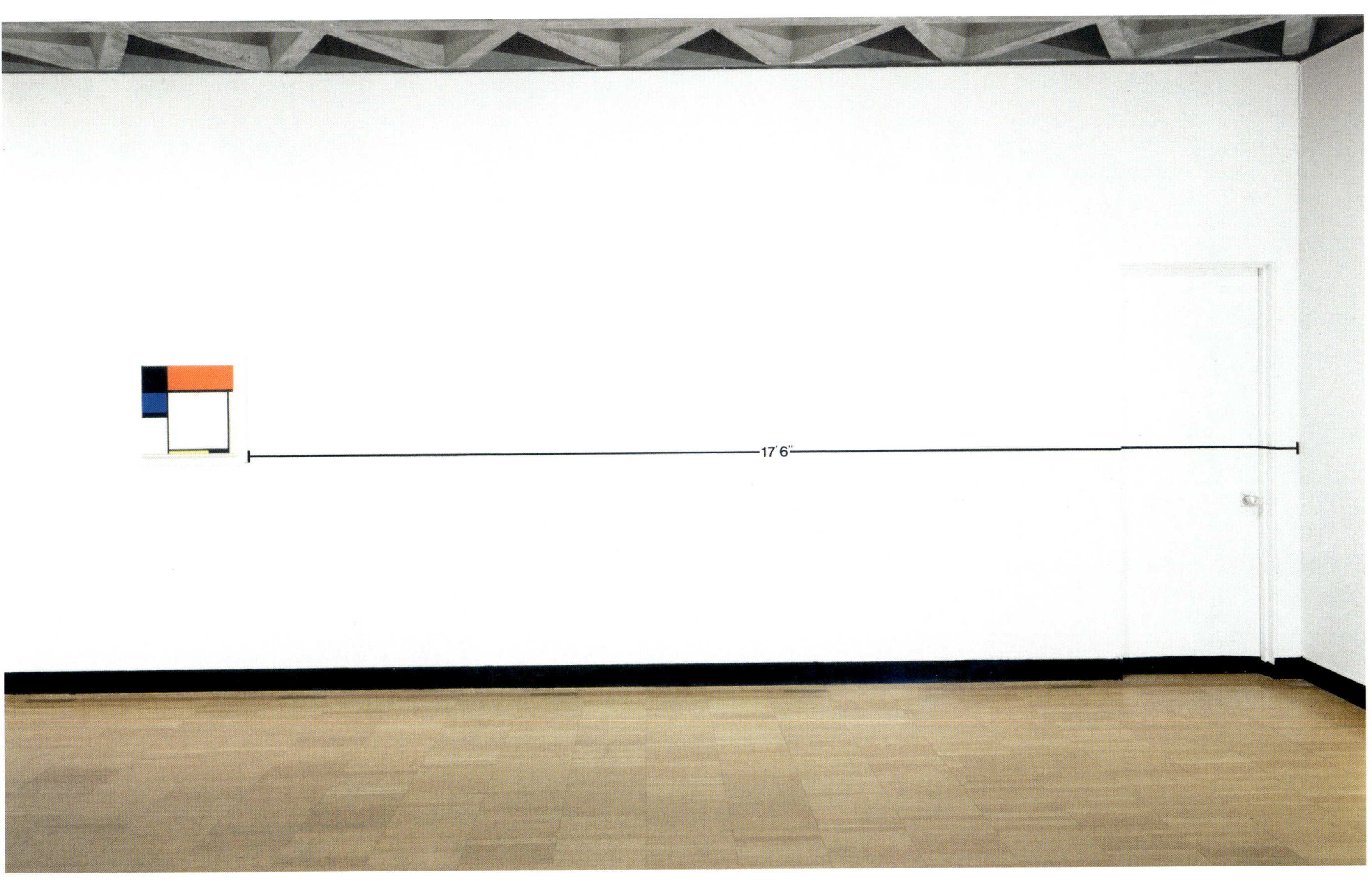
17' 6"

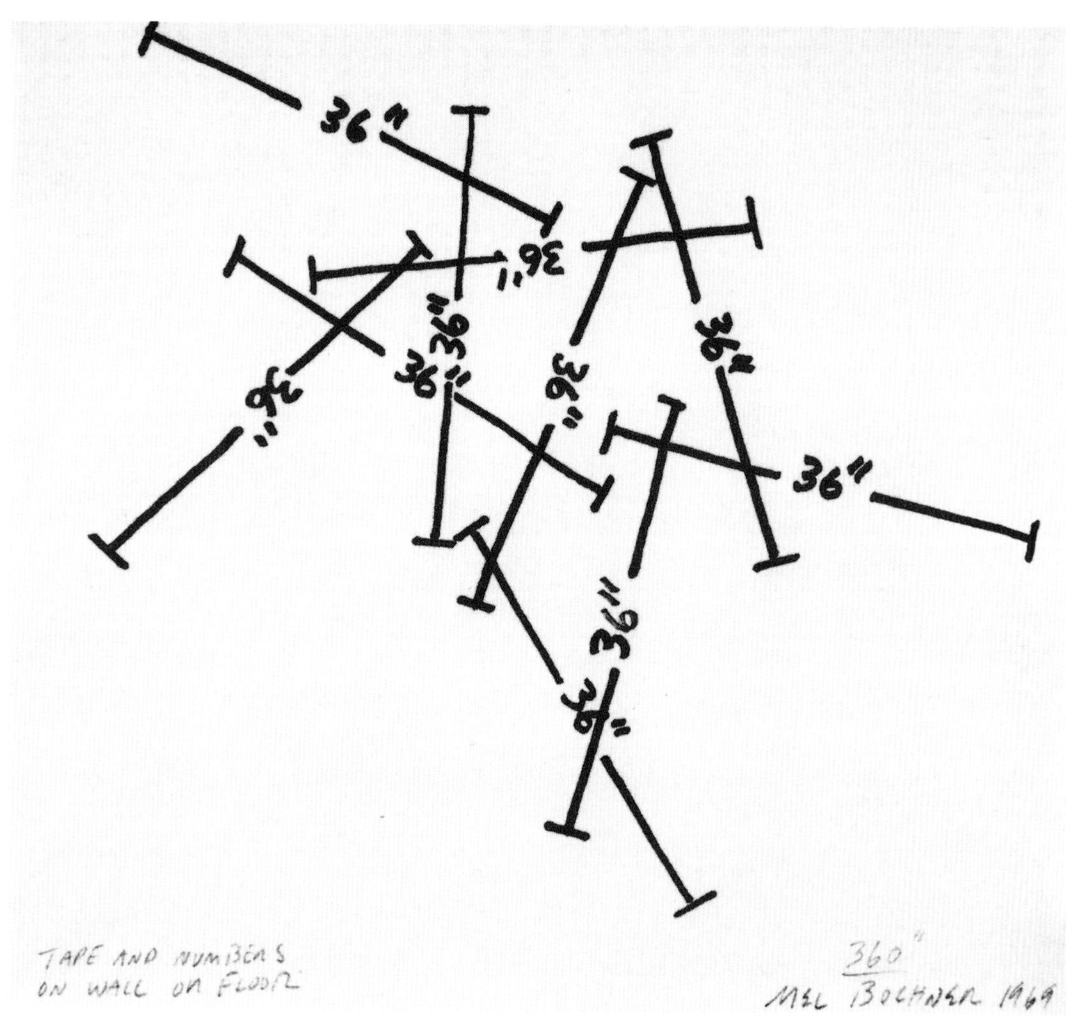

360 Inches (Study for Installation), 1969
Ink on paper
6¾ × 7¼ inches
Private collection

Untitled (Forgoing the Support), 1969
Ink on paper
11 × 8½ inches

forgoing the support

floor piece

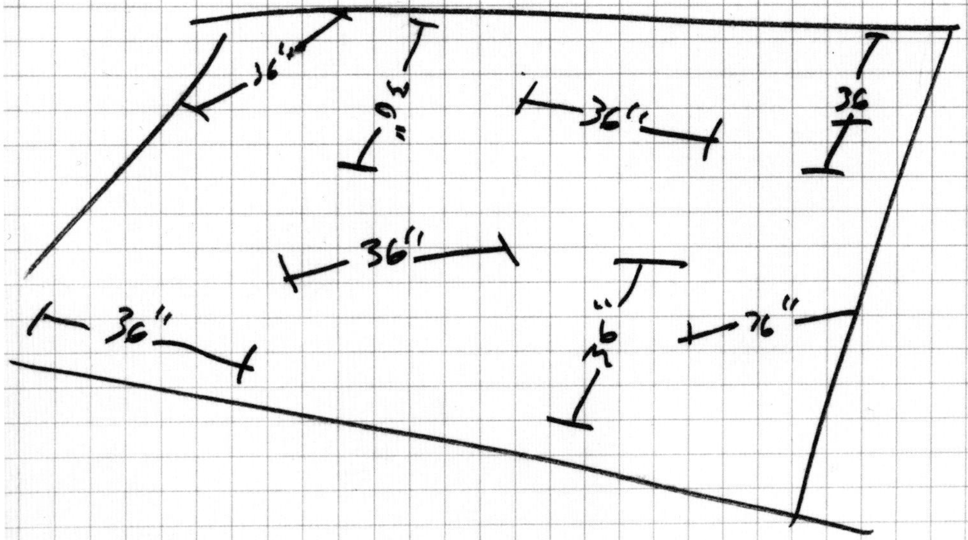

36"

3'6"

36"

36

36"

36"

36"

3'6"

find image for
Malcolm

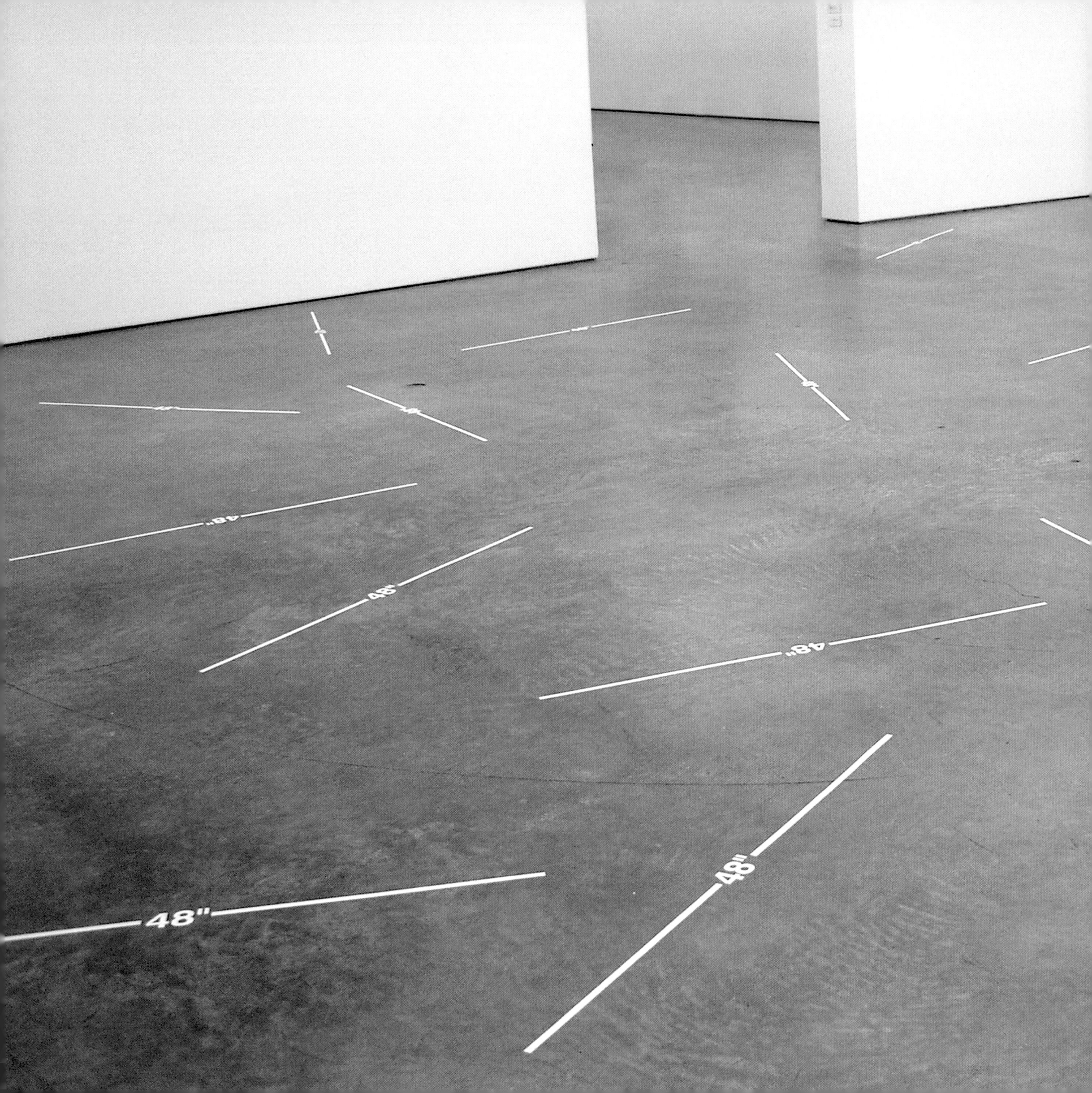
48"
48"
48"

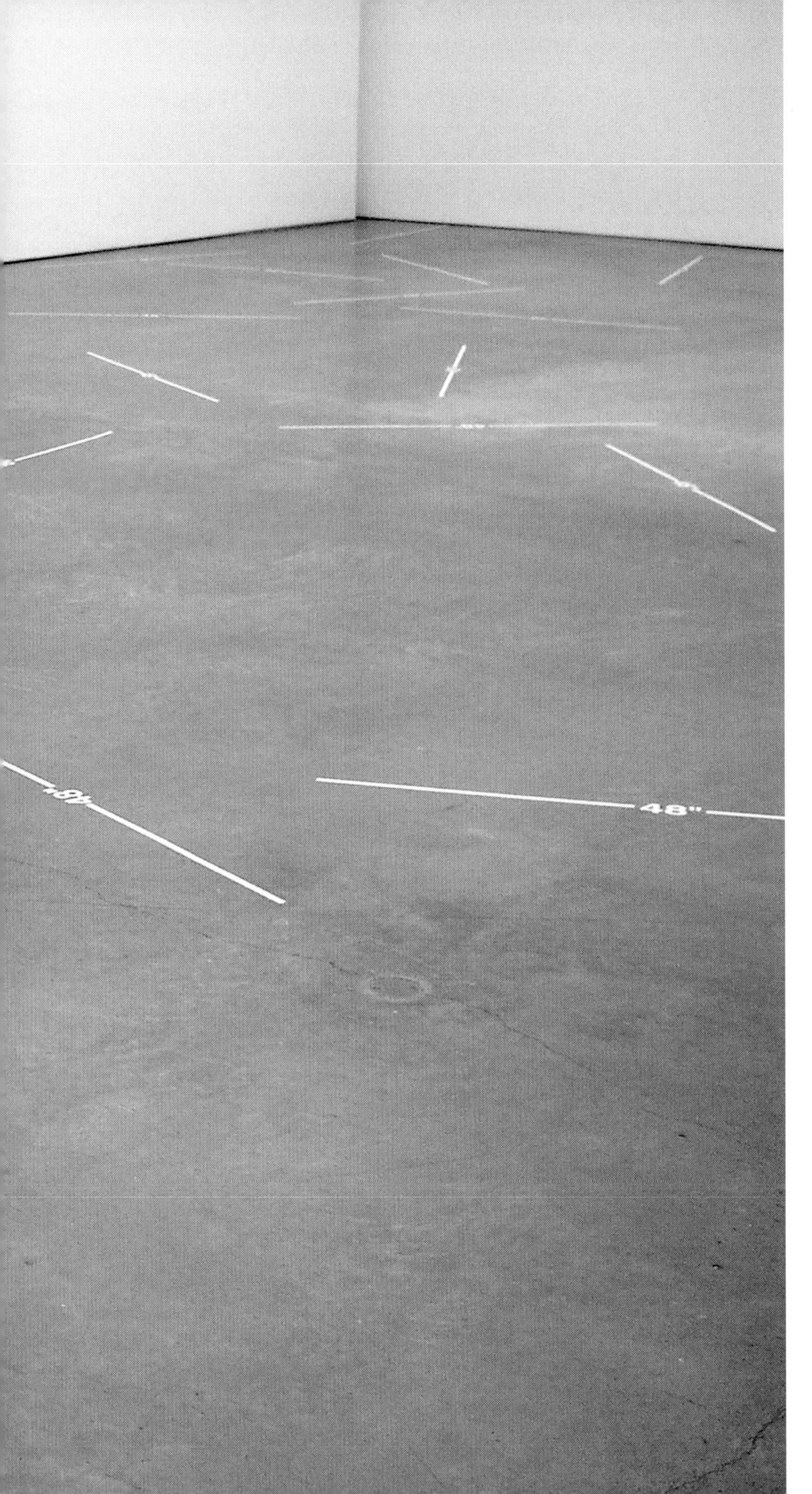

48 Inches (Around the Floor), 1969

Letraset and tape on floor

Installation view, *Instructure*, Hessel Museum of Art, Center for Curatorial Studies at Bard College, Annandale-on-Hudson, New York, 2003

Measurement: 1–10 Feet, 1969–70

Letraset and tape on wall

Installation view, *measurements*, Société, Brussels, 2018

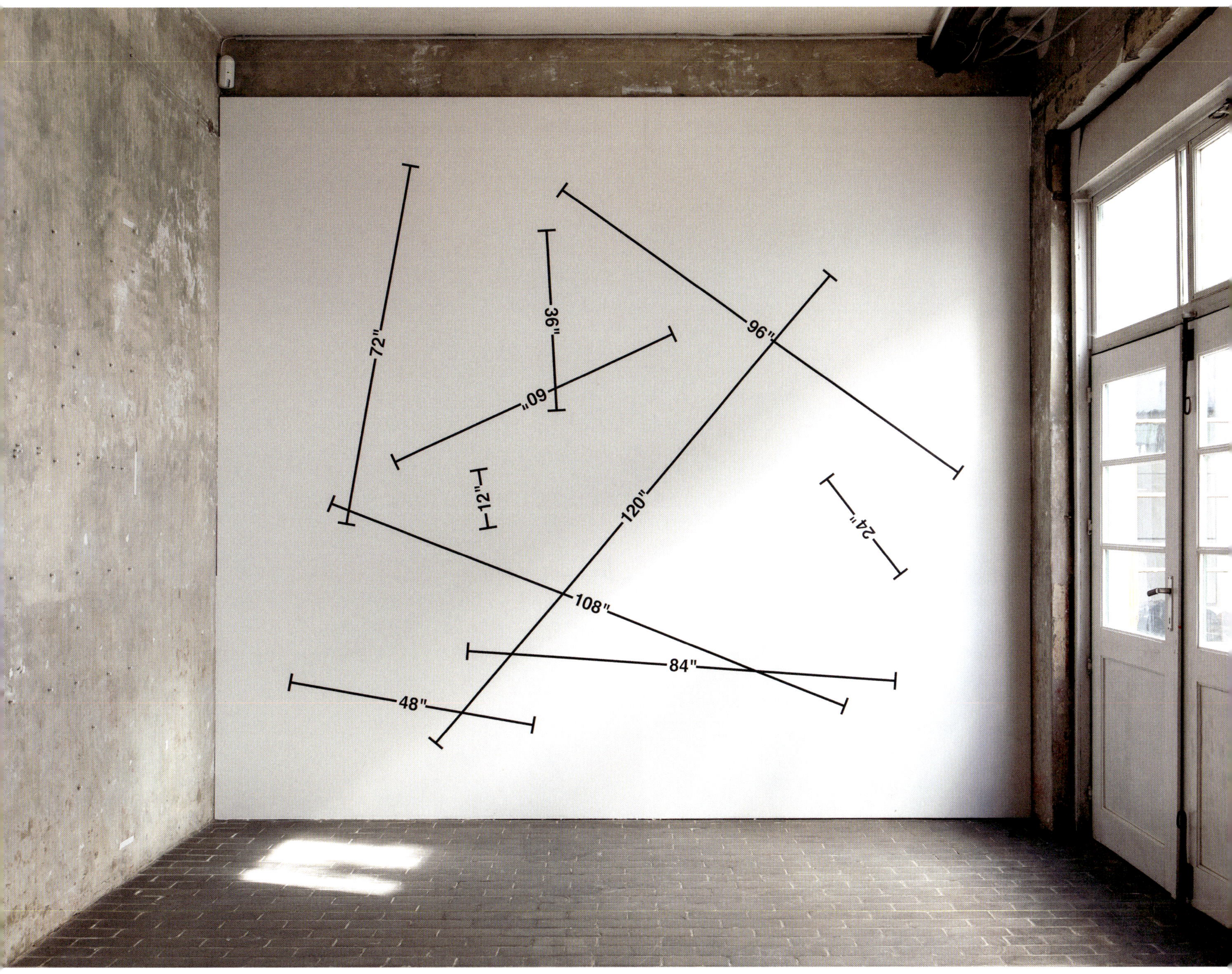
72"
36"
96"
60"
12"
120"
24"
108"
84"
48"

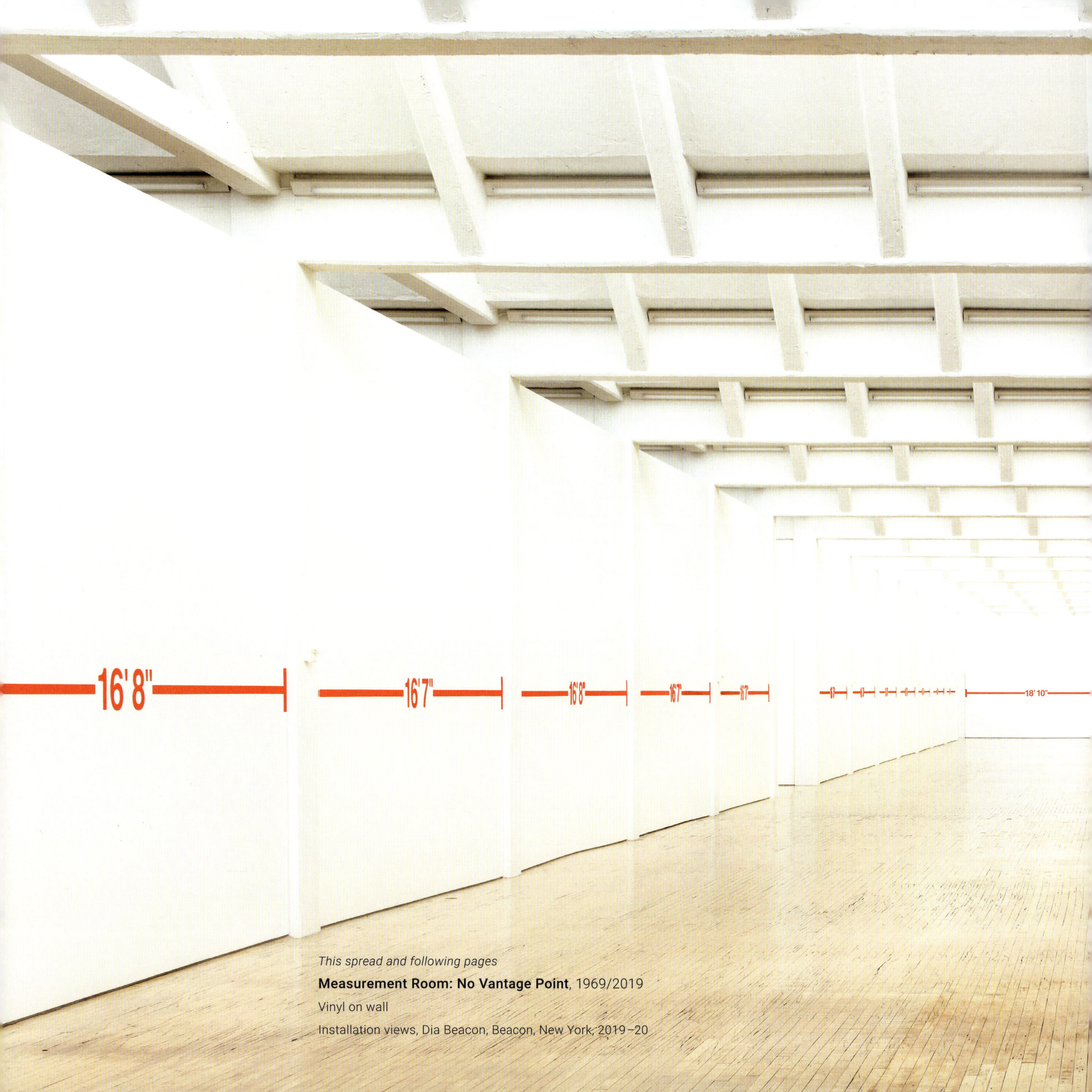

This spread and following pages

Measurement Room: No Vantage Point, 1969/2019

Vinyl on wall

Installation views, Dia Beacon, Beacon, New York, 2019–20

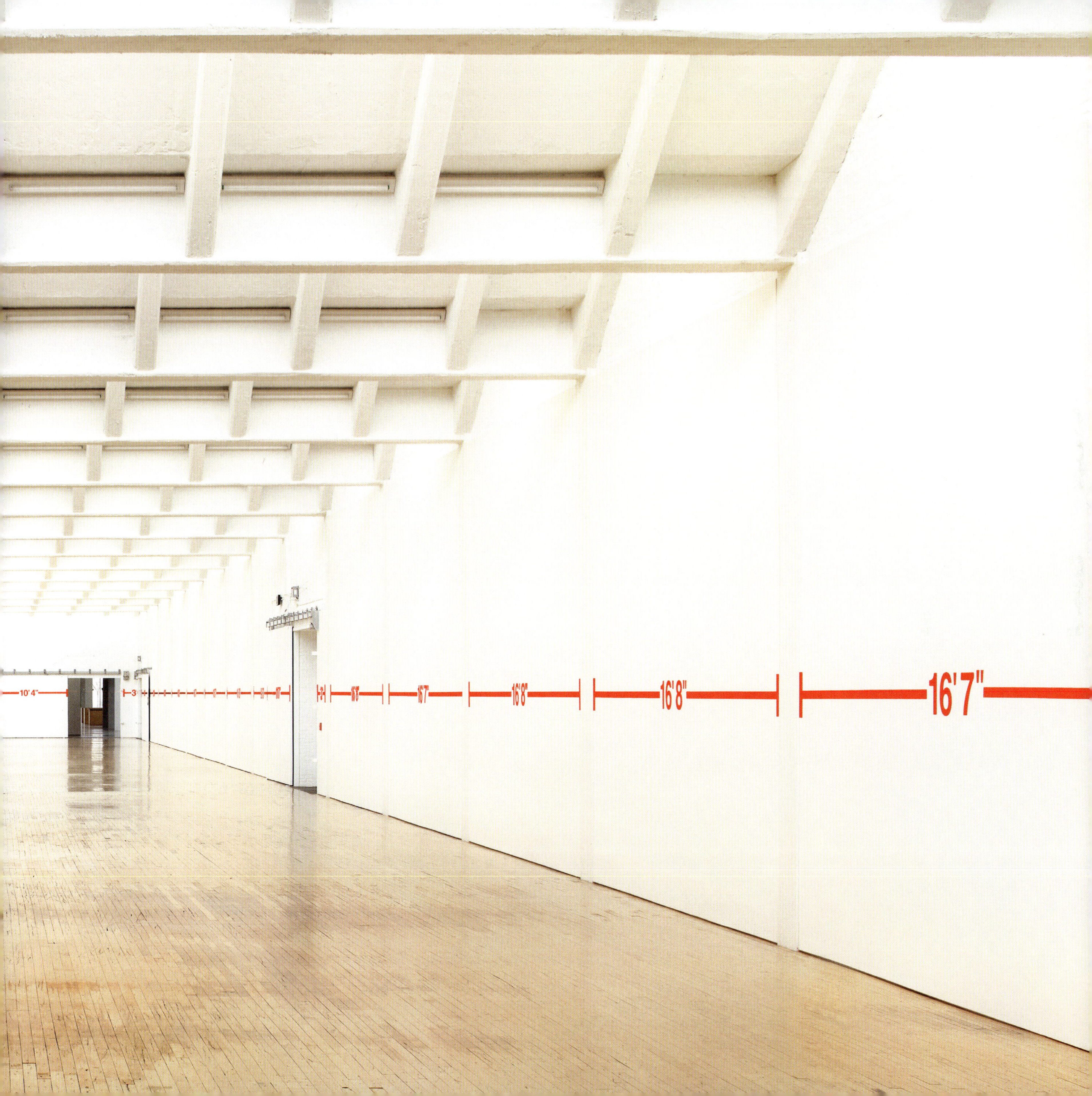
10' 4"
3
16'8"
16'7"
16'8"
16'8"
16'7"

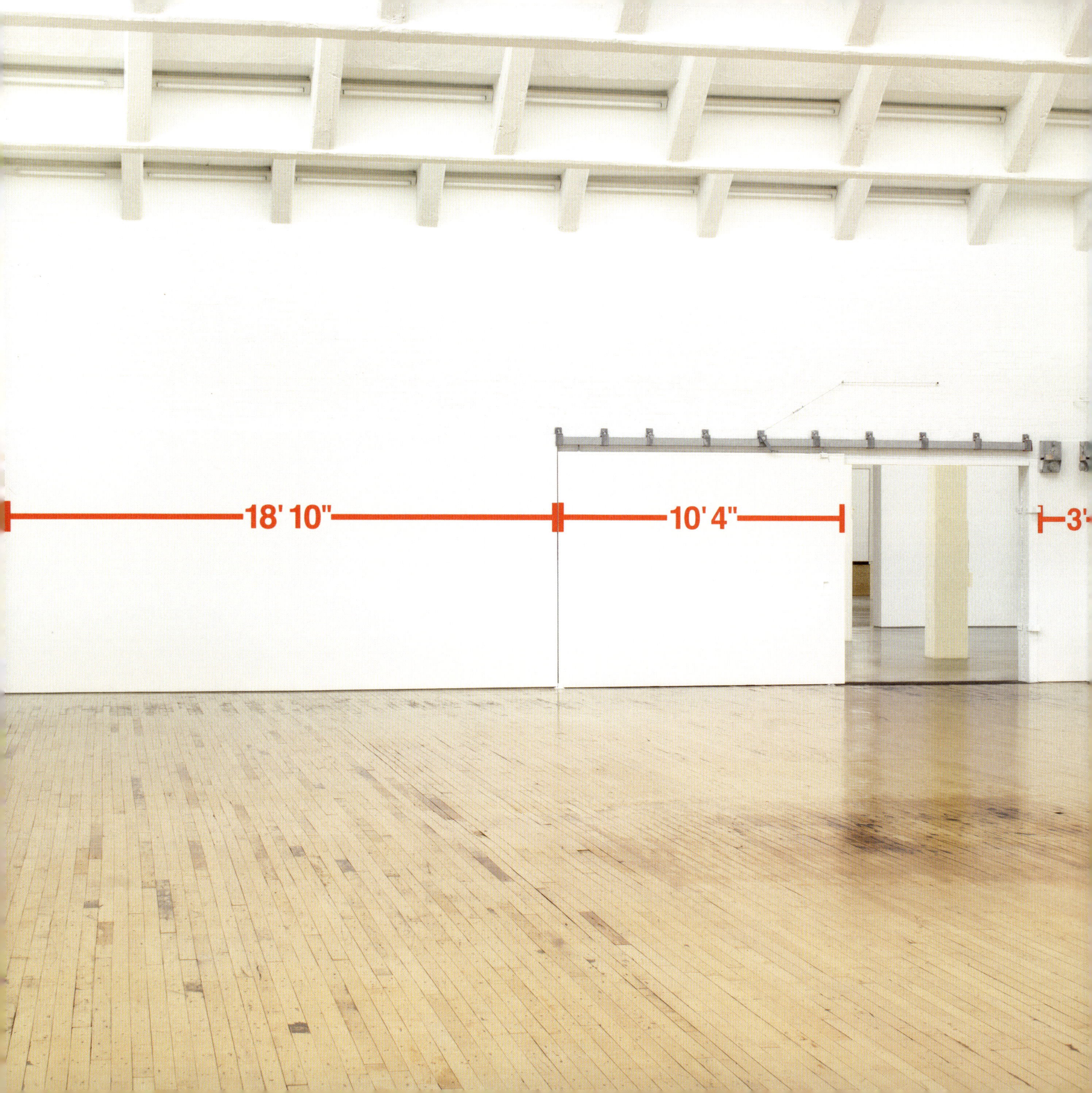
18' 10"
10' 4"
3'

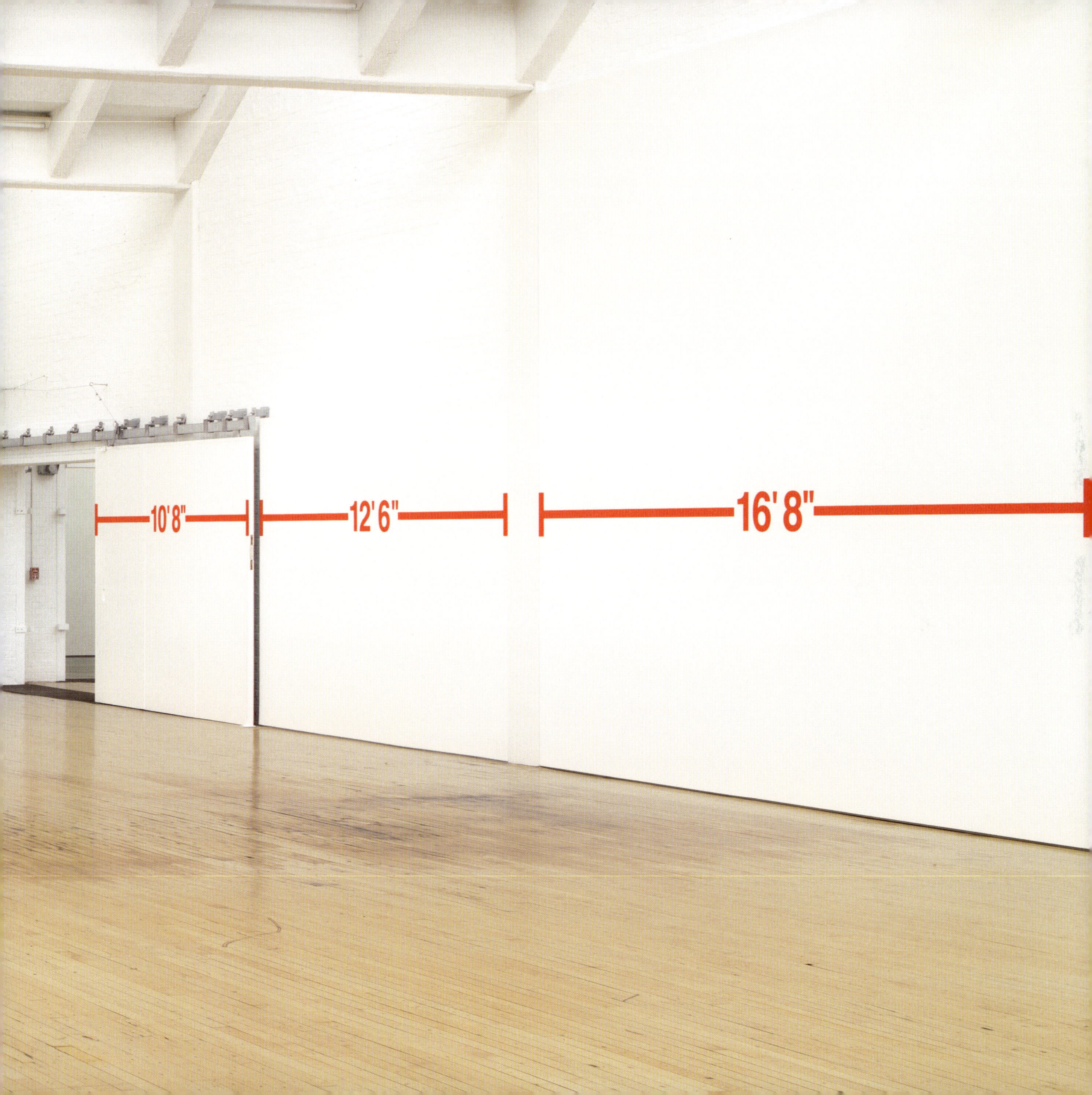
10'8"
12'6"
16'8"

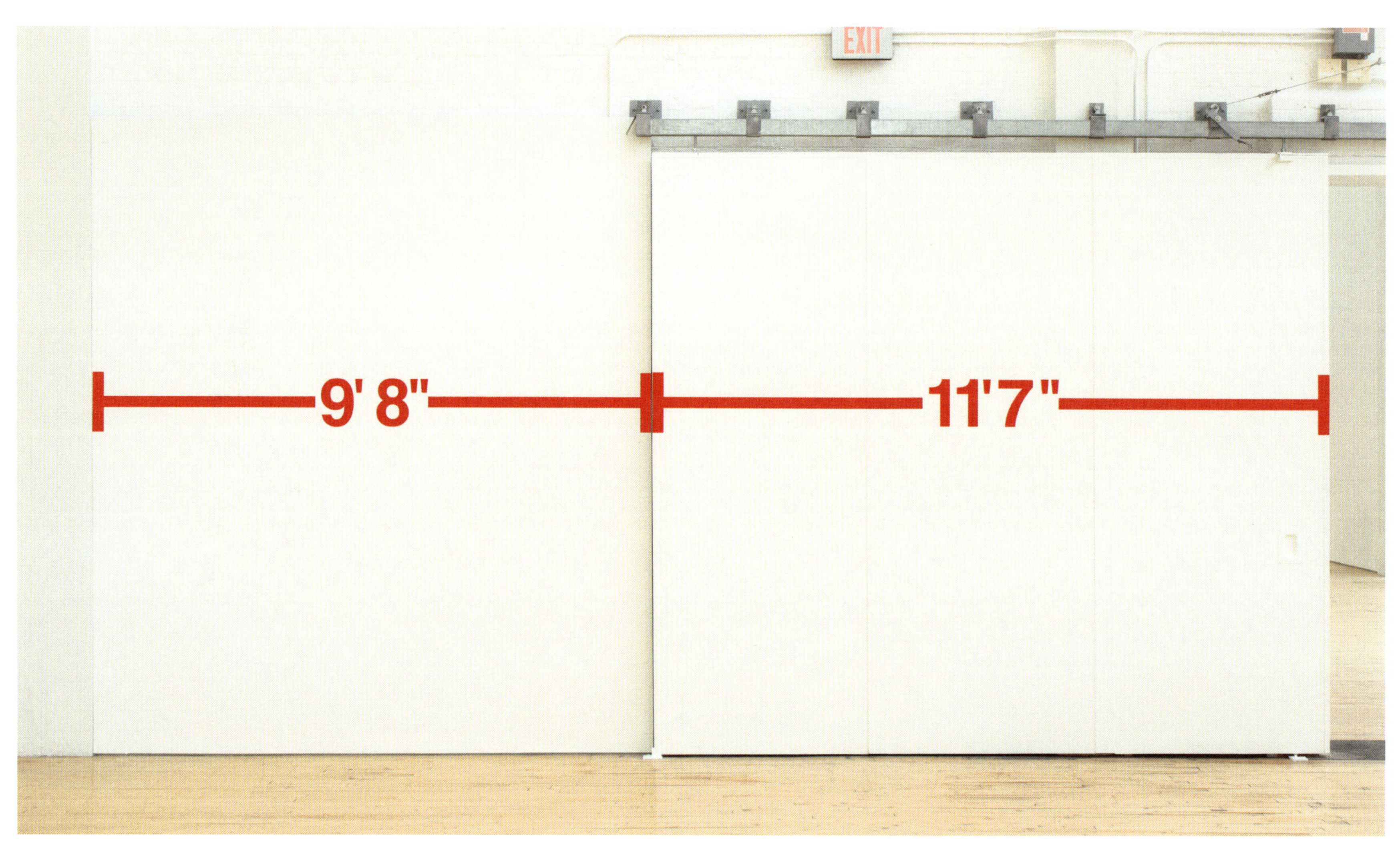
EXIT
9' 8"
11'7"

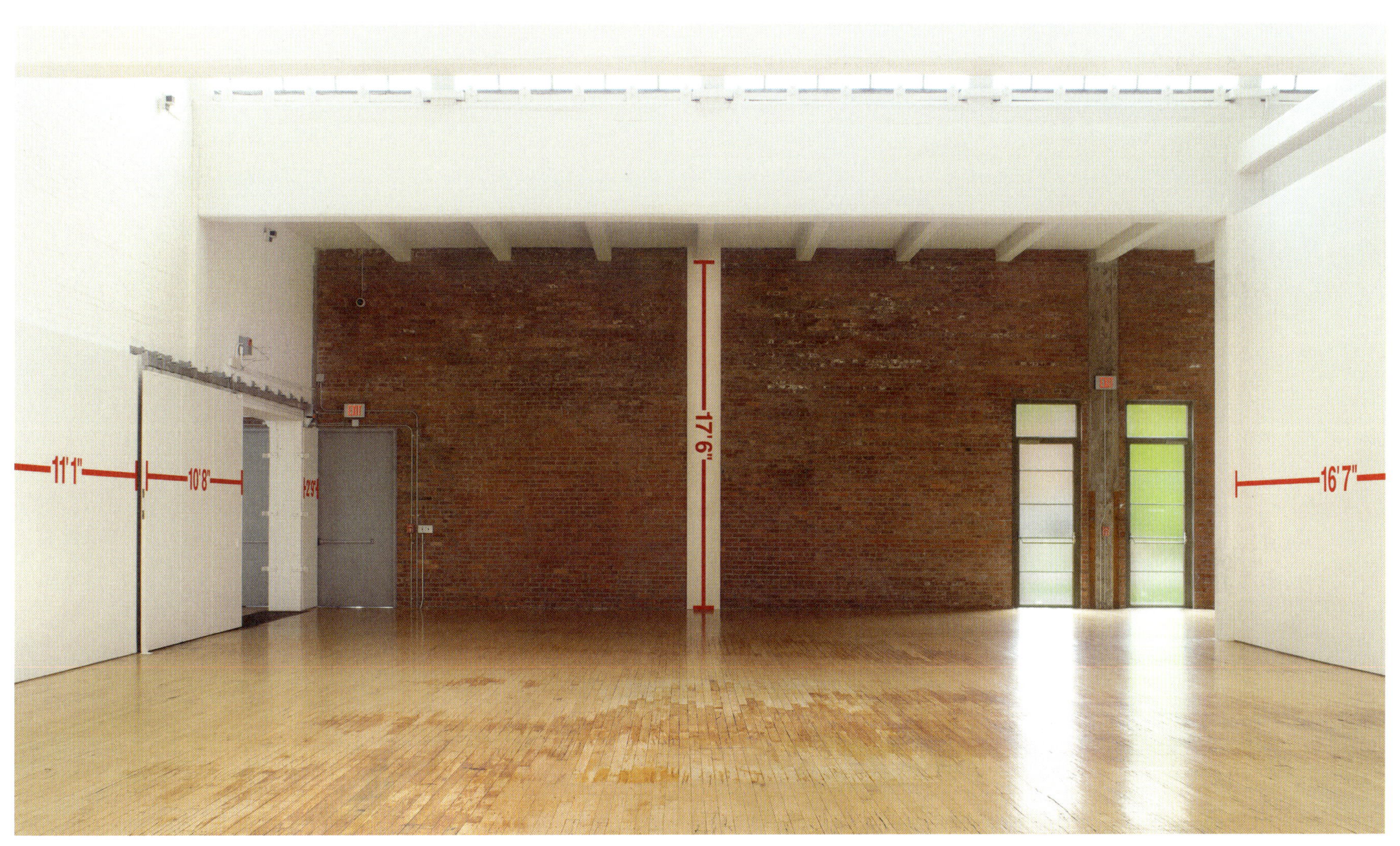
11'1"
10'8"
17'6"
16'7"

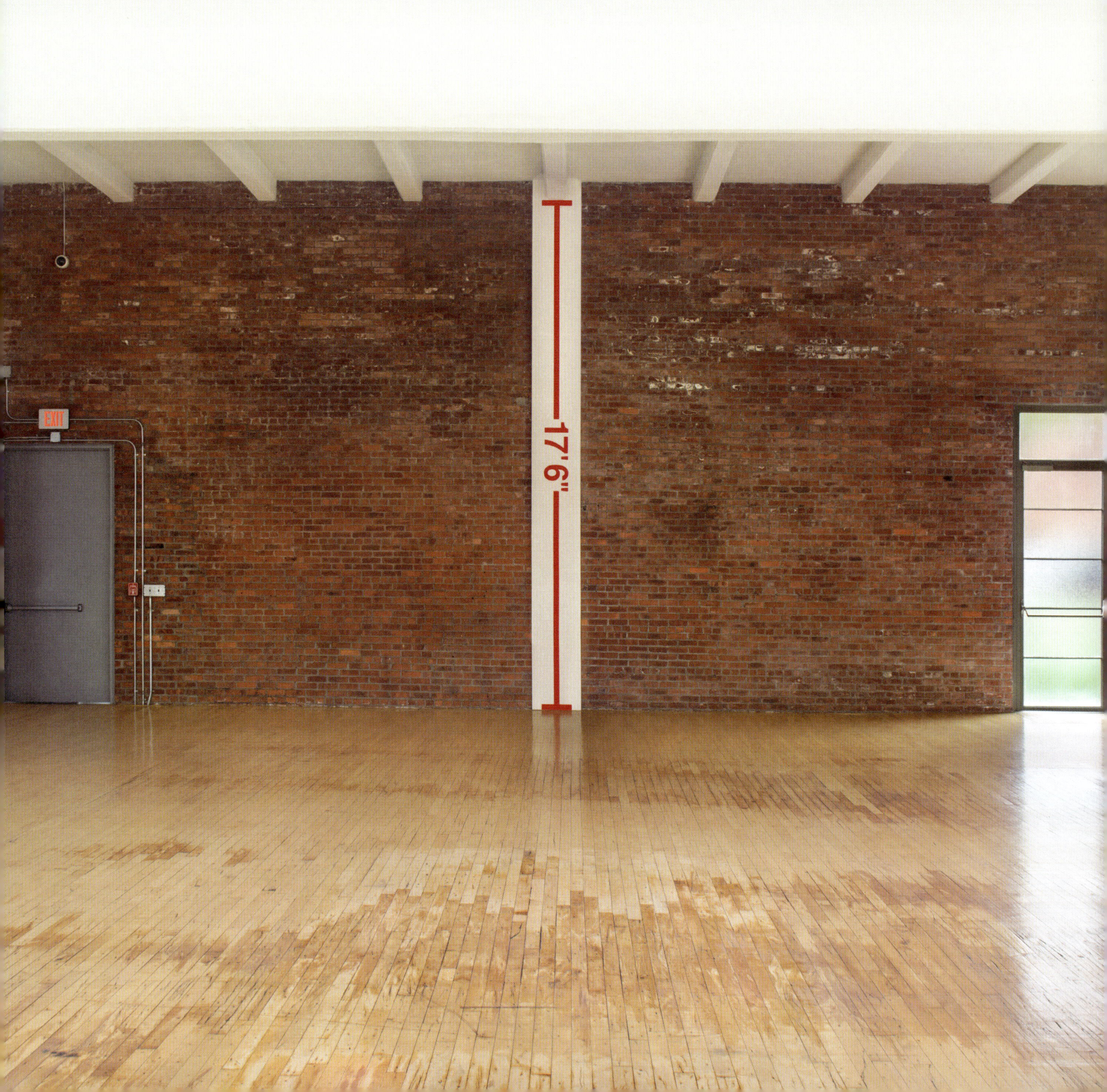
EXIT
17'6"

"The World as I Found It": Mel Bochner's Measuring without a Vantage Point

Alexis Lowry

> *If I wrote a book called* The World as I found it, *I should have to include a report on my body, and should have to say which parts were subordinate to my will, and which were not, etc., this being a method of isolating the subject, or rather of showing that in an important sense there is no subject; for it alone could* not *be mentioned in that book.*
>
> —Ludwig Wittgenstein, *Tractatus Logico-Philosophicus* (1921)

Measurement by definition implies a comparison, and every measurement is a ratio of values or a measurement of something. This inherent mutability exists in opposition to the fact that measurements are also the skeleton or structure of modern social order. They are the instruments of power by which society rationalizes the world into predictable units of value. The artist Mel Bochner has been preoccupied with this seeming paradox since 1968, when he conceived of the Measurement series. This unfolding body of work, brought together for the first time in this volume, explores questions of mathematical and perceptual relativity.

Bochner's interest in the relational nature of measurement was first cultivated when he was an artist-in-residence at the Singer Laboratories in New Jersey during the fall of 1968, as part of artist Robert Rauschenberg and engineer Billy Klüver's E.A.T. (Experiments in Art and Technology) program, which invited artists to collaborate with scientists and engineers. He began his residency at Singer when the company shifted its focus away from sewing machines to calculators, computer flight simulators, and GPS systems. This change in business strategy landed Singer at the forefront of an international explosion in technologies of surveillance and mapping. During this time many artists and cultural theorists believed that the changing nature of communication technology posed an existential threat to the physical experience of real space. This turn toward spatial concerns formed the backdrop of Bochner's regular meetings with Singer engineers, mathematicians, and physicists, where discussions on topics of mutual interest ranged from color theory to binary code.[1] Soon Bochner began to realize that everything came down to one issue: "verification."[2] Skeptical of this type of scientific absolutism and its far-reaching consequences, the artist started to explore ways of disrupting this positivist logic. In one instance, Bochner surreptitiously measured random sections of the laboratory's facilities by using rub-on Letraset type and leaving these spatial interventions for his colleagues to discover, such as twelve inches marked out on the floor tiles or ten inches marked from the tip of an aerosol can to the edge of a wall (see pp. 18–19).[3] Bochner's measurements, though exact, were also comically illogical, and while he addressed the limits of the use-value of a standardized spatial system, he consequently engendered a sense of the uncanny.

Following his artist residency at Singer, Bochner continued to interrogate the relationship between quantifiable sets of data and real spatial encounters by measuring everything he could get his hands on, from the objects in his studio—standard sheets of paper, boxes, and lines and angles he had demarcated—to his own limbs and torso or, as the philosopher Ludwig Wittgenstein might have said, "the world as he found it." Bochner's work in this Measurement series eventually grew in scope and culminated with the environmentally encompassing *Measurement: Room* (1969), which carefully mapped the dimensions of a gallery's walls across its surfaces with tape and Letraset numbers. *Measurement: Room* was originally produced as part of his solo exhibition, *Measurements*, at Galerie Heiner Friedrich in Munich in May 1969 (Heiner Friedrich would go on to cofound Dia Art Foundation in 1974). The show explored the relationship between the numerical systems used to rationalize the built environment and actual perceptually contingent experiences of space. As the artist recently explained, "What I realized I needed to do was expose the hidden regime of architecture, to make it reveal itself."[4] The *Measurement: Room* transformed the gallery into a three-dimensional blueprint—a projection of spatial volumes—that each viewer reconciled with the physical structures around them. Standing before a window marked as seven feet high, the adjacent five-foot-wide doorframe was obscured; looking at a wall that was labeled ten feet by ten inches in length, the windows receded to the background. The room was only envisioned through movement as viewers encountered the space in relationship to their own size and through Bochner's denotations.

Now considered an important touchstone of Conceptual art, the *Measurement: Room*, along with its shifting phenomenological focus, was not immediately understood or appreciated by all. In a revealing encounter, the one critic who came to review the show (from the nationally distributed German newspaper *Frankfurter Allgemeine Zeitung*) determined the work was impossible to appraise because Bochner had rendered his matrix in the Anglo-American measurement system of feet and inches. This was a foreign language to the European critic, who was accustomed to the metric system, which uses a different standard to calculate lengths. Essentially, it was the confrontation of two incommensurable systems. With the purported spatial veracity of the newly mapped space lost in translation, the critic, like the earlier Singer scientists who were without a means of verification, deemed it impossible to review the work, and feeling indignant, he departed. Despite the seeming absurdity of the situation, Bochner appreciated that the critic rightly (if subconsciously and intuitively) understood that the *Measurement: Room* was, in fact, about the subjectivity of spatial encounters. The social theorist Andrea Mubi Brighenti writes, "Making measures is a way of making *meaning* and, concurrently, of making meaning *visible*."[5] Carefully articulating the distances between windows and moldings and doors and walls, Bochner's installation visualizes the structural divisions whose administrative function is to regulate and condition our social and spatial lives, and in turn his installation situates the production of their meaning with each visitor.

Not long after, the artist proposed a second project to Friedrich called *No Vantage Point: Eye Level Cross-Section of a Room*. The *Measurement: Room* had presented an index of architectural features that fractured the viewer's perception of the exhibition space as a whole; it dispersed the "art" object throughout the gallery by transposing the center of the work onto the mobile visitor who was surrounded by notations.[6] Alternatively, *No Vantage Point* would bind these walls perceptually back together by tracing a red perimeter line around the room. Even though this exhibition was never realized, it, too, would have positioned each viewer centrally by untethering the aesthetic experience from any single perspective. The red line was evenly marked no matter which way a viewer looked. Bochner has noted, "For me, an essential part of this work's meaning is the experience of the room's emptiness."[7]

Commissioned by Dia Art Foundation on the occasion of the fiftieth anniversary of *Measurement: Room* and *No Vantage Point*, Bochner's new work, *Measurement Room: No Vantage Point*, brings together elements of the earlier works to create the largest installation of the Measurement series to date. The new work consists of a thick red line broken by numerical intervals that circumscribe and measure the walls of a central gallery at Dia Beacon. At first glance the repetitious bays appear uniform in size, but as the viewer moves through the space, Bochner exposes the subtle variances between them—often only a matter of inches—which would otherwise be invisible to the naked eye. While the walls fluctuate, the line runs evenly across at a six-foot height, Bochner's own eye level, or what he calls his "horizon line," and establishes a kind of control for the visitors to measure their experience of the space. In this sense, Bochner positions the viewers themselves as their own measuring instruments.

Measurement Room: No Vantage Point addresses the friction produced between the body as a measurement of space and other metrics of identity. The Measurement series was conceived at a moment when perceptual processes came under investigation by a range of artists who were concerned with the administration of modern space, and the ways in which technologies of mapping and communication dematerialize or subordinate the experience of real space. In today's digital era, the "social structures" that condition our daily lives are more "often disguised beneath an abstract, instrumental space, or incarcerated in the coordinates of computer mapping."[8] As our social relations are increasingly mediated by apps and avatars, the embodied knowledge that Bochner cultivates in the viewer is a reminder that we are each a measure of the physical world.

The epigraph is from Ludwig Wittgenstein, *Tractatus Logico-Philosophicus*, trans. D. F. Pears and B. F. McGuinness (London: Routledge and Kegan Paul, 1961), section 5.631, p. 117.

1 Edward W. Soja describes what he calls a "spatial turn" in critical theory throughout *Postmodern Geographies: The Reassertion of Space in Critical Social Theory* (New York: Verso, 1989).

2 "There is no communication without an agreed-upon means of verification. Communication is verification, and verification is measurement." Mel Bochner, *Singer Notes, 1968* (Paris: mfc-michèle didier, 2017), n.p.

3 Bochner describes these first measurement works in ibid.

4 Ibid.

5 Andrea Mubi Brighenti, "The Social Life of Measures: Conceptualizing Measure-Value Environments," *Theory, Culture & Society* 35, no. 1 (January 2018), p. 28.

6 Bochner, *Singer Notes, 1968*, n.p.

7 Bochner in conversation with the author, October 7, 2019.

8 J. B. Harley, *The New Nature of Maps: Essays in the History of Cartography,* ed. Paul Laxton (Baltimore: Johns Hopkins University Press, 2002), p. 156.

I Concede the Whole Room, 1969

Ink on offset lithograph

6 × 4 inches

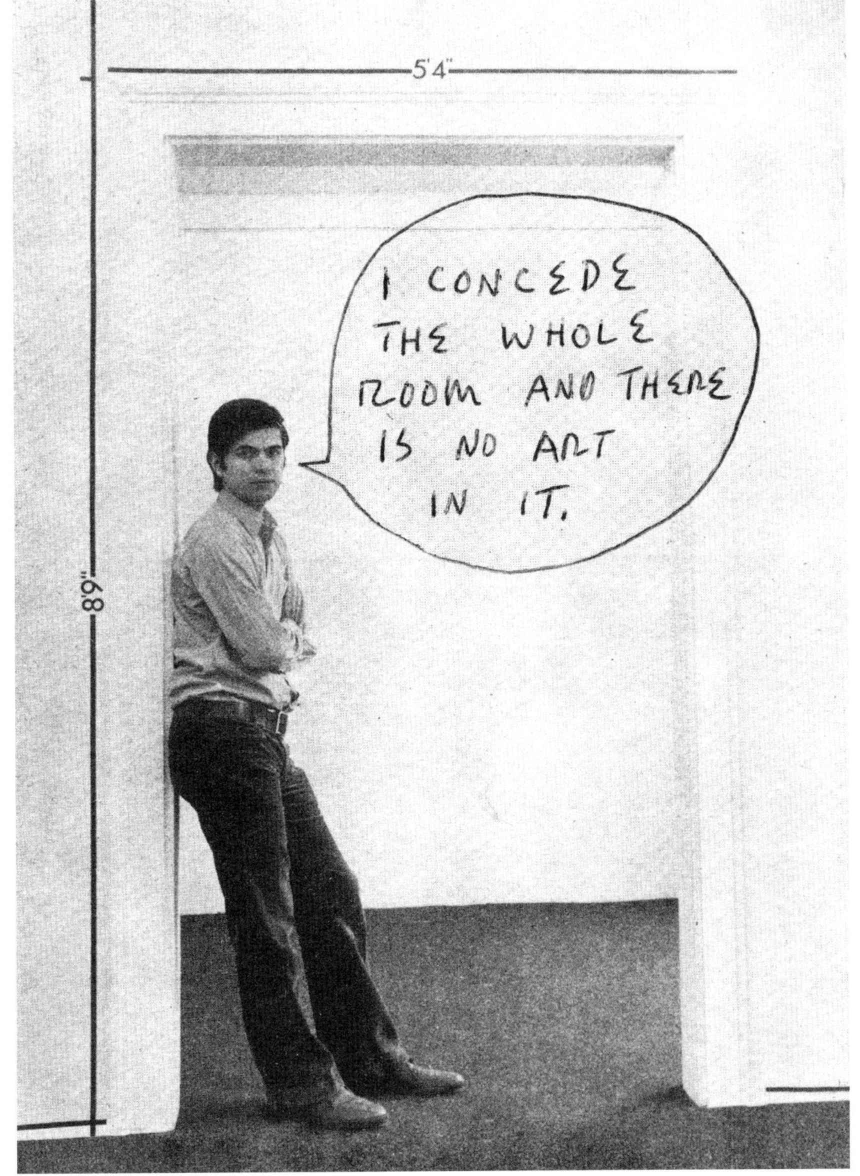
5'4"
8'9"
I CONCEDE THE WHOLE ROOM AND THERE IS NO ART IN IT.

This book was published on the occasion of the exhibition *Mel Bochner* at Dia Beacon, Beacon, New York, November 9, 2019–May 9, 2021.

Mel Bochner is made possible by generous support from the Ampersand Foundation. Additional support is provided by Jill and Peter Kraus, Simon Lee, and Susan and Larry Marx.

Support for the publication is provided by Lisa and Tom Blumenthal; Peter Freeman, Inc.; Evelyn and David Lasry/ Two Palms, New York; and Marc Selwyn Fine Art.

First printing, 2020

Dia Art Foundation
535 West 22nd Street
New York, NY 10011
diaart.org

Distributed by ARTBOOK | D.A.P.
75 Broad Street, Suite 630
New York, NY 10004
T: (212) 627-1999
F: (212) 627-9484
artbook.com

Design: Mel Bochner with Phil Kovacevich and James Powers
Editors: Kamilah N. Foreman, Elizabeth Franzen, and Sophia Larigakis
Rights and reproduction: Mollie Bernstein

Typeset in Roboto and Minion Pro
Printed on 150 gsm GardaPat bianka
Printed and bound in Belgium by die Keure

Jacket illustration: Installation view, *Measurements*, Galerie Heiner Friedrich, Munich, 1969

Photo Credits
Unless otherwise noted, all works collection of the artist. All works by Mel Bochner and all photos © Mel Bochner, courtesy the artist

Page 31, Photo: Pelka/Noble; page 100, © The Museum of Modern Art, New York; pages 103–07, Photo: Shunk-Kender. © J. Paul Getty Trust, courtesy Getty Research Institute, Los Angeles; pages 112–13, Photo: Chris Kendall, courtesy CCS Bard Library & Archives, Bard College; pages 116–22, Photo: Bill Jacobson Studio, New York, courtesy Dia Art Foundation, New York

ISBN 978-0-944521-90-8

Library of Congress Number: 2019955240